Spirit of the Red Stick Women

By Debra Hughey

Wake Forest, NC

www.scuppernongpress.com

Spirit of the Red Stick Women

©2017 Debra Hughey

First Printing

The Scuppernong Press
PO Box 1724
Wake Forest, NC 27588
www.scuppernongpress.com

Cover and book design by Frank B. Powell, III

All rights reserved. Printed in the United States of America.

No part of this book may be reproduced or transmitted in any form or by any means, electronic or mechanical, including photocopying, recording, or by any information and storage and retrieval system, without written permission from the editor and/or publisher.

International Standard Book Number ISBN 978-1-942806-10-3

Library of Congress Control Number: 2017946965

Table of Contents

Foreword 1
Chapter One 3
Chapter Two 9
Chapter Three..11
Chapter Four 15
Chapter Five..19
Chapter Six..23
Chapter Seven 25
Chapter Eight 29
Chapter Nine 31
Chapter Ten 35
Chapter Eleven...37
Chapter Twelve 39
Chapter Thirteen 41
Chapter Fourteen...45
Chapter Fifteen...49
Chapter Sixteen..53
Chapter Seventeen 55
Chapter Eighteen..57
Chapter Nineteen 61
Chapter Twenty 63
Chapter Twenty-One..67
Chapter Twenty-Two..69
Chapter Twenty-Three 71
Chapter Twenty-Four...75
Chapter Twenty-Five..77
Chapter Twenty-Six..79

Chapter Twenty-Seven ... 81
Chapter Twenty-Eight ... 83
Chapter Twenty-Nine ... 89
Chapter Thirty ... 91
Chapter Thirty-One ... 93
Chapter Thirty-Two ... 97
Chapter Thirty-Three ... 101
Chapter Thirty-Four ... 103
Chapter Thirty-Five ... 105
Chapter Thirty-Six ... 107
Chapter Thirty-Seven ... 111
Chapter Thirty-Eight ... 115
Chapter Thirty-Nine ... 119
Chapter Forty ... 123
Chapter Forty-One ... 127
Chapter Forty-Two ... 131
Chapter Forty-Three ... 133
Chapter Forty-Four ... 137
Chapter Forty-Five ... 139
Chapter Forty-Six ... 143
Chapter Forty-Seven ... 147
Chapter Forty-Eight ... 151
Chapter Forty-Nine ... 153
Chapter Fifty ... 155
Epilogue ... 157
Acknowledgements ... 158
Glossary of Creek Words ... 159
Photos ... 160
Map ... 176

Foreword

The Hillabee people had heard the melancholy call of the owl. They had experienced much sadness and grief and knew the owl's cry had been an omen for the future.

The Owl and the Horseshoe is a story of a Red Stick family and the tragic events leading up to the great battle at the Horseshoe. A battle which would forever change the lives of not only the Hillabee, but also all Creek people.

Spirit of the Red Stick Women is the sequel to *The Owl and the Horseshoe*. This story tells of the lives of the family after the Horseshoe. A great majority of Creek Warriors at the battle did not live to see the sun set on that day. What would happen to their women and children?

As with *The Owl and the Horseshoe, Spirit of the Red Stick Women* is based on historical events, the few that are available. Many of the same characters combined with the new, create an exciting but unexpected turn of events. While the plight of the women continues to be filled with extreme hardship and grief, they will depend on the strength of the grandmothers and they will survive.

Return now to the Tallapoosa. The day is March 28, 1814. Experience the emotional heartaches and learn of the *Spirit of the Red Stick Women.*

After the Horsehoe
Chapter One

Sunflower Woman was the first to notice the dozens of death birds circling high in the afternoon sky. Had the chilling wind blown from the opposite direction, the smell of blood of the slain warriors would have filled the air. Many of the dead had been thrown into the rapid water of the Tallapoosa River. Some had been overlooked by the white soldiers in their haste to gather their own dead and to leave the area. The area of the horseshoe, where only the day before so many had seen the sun for the last time.

Sunflower Woman and her daughter, Little Flower, her grandchildren, Little Deer, Red Fox and forty-six of the women and children followed six Creek warriors down the worn path. Another woman, having seen the ugly birds of death, began keening. Soon the sounds of sorrow came from all of the women and the children responding to the pain of their mothers, began to cry. The beautiful black hair of the women had already been cropped and bloody scratches were still visible on the arms of many. Each woman and child on the path had lost a loved one, a husband, a son, a father or a brother in the battle which had occurred. Knowing they were near the site of Tohopeka, the group lost all control of their pent-up emotions. The six warriors watched helplessly as the group continued their crying and keening as the sun moved to a lower point in the sky. The warriors understood their sorrow, they too had lost friends in the battle, the battle of which they had been a part. They were White Sticks from the town of Coweta and the responsibility of taking this small group of the three-hundred and fifty other captives to their town had been assigned to them.

The warriors realized they had no time to waste, the trip to the Chattahoochee would take several suns and they knew the small supply of corn and bad meat the white soldiers had rationed would not be enough. They also knew that food supplies from the small towns that dotted the river had been seized for the use of the white army or had been destroyed. They knew these people would be hungry.

Since leaving the encampment at Emuckfau Creek, where the captives had been taken, the beautiful older woman called Sunflower Woman had assumed the position of leader. She had heard the white officers talking and she knew this group was first being taken down-river to Tuckabatchee Town and from there some would continue on to Coweta. She realized there was not enough food. Before departing for the journey she had also heard the white soldiers laugh as they talked of taking all of the food supplies from the savage people.

Sunflower Woman was well aware that she and the others could overtake the White Stick Warriors at any time and be free, but where would they go and what would they do? Most, if not all of their men where dead and the towns had all been burned. She also guessed and was correct that some of the white army was still nearby. These savage women must not be allowed to reunite with any of the Red Stick warriors that might have eluded the soldiers.

Sunflower Woman turned to face the large group of keening women. As she looked into the eyes of her family and friends, she experienced a strange emotion, one that made her visibly tremble. Watching their leader, one by one, the keening women became silent. With tears streaming down the face that had seen many suns and much sorrow, Sunflower Woman began to slowly speak. "My family and my friends. Be still. Listen. Do you not also hear and feel the spirit of the brave warriors, of our husbands, our fathers and our sons who no longer live. They are now on the path that leads to the home of the Great Spirit, the Giver of Breath. They are no longer with us, no more will we hear their laughter or feel their touch." Her voice breaking, Sunflower Woman paused as she remembered the loving embrace of her husband as he bid her farewell only the day before. "We stand now just a short distance away from where they saw the sun for the last time. They vowed to protect us and to save the land of our grandfathers. They fought as Creek warriors. We are Creek women and we will fight to preserve their spirit for as long as we see the rising of the sun. We will go now to Tuckabatchee Town and on to the river of Flowered Rocks if we are ordered to do so. We will live so that our warriors will not have died for a cause that was lost."

As if on cue from their leader, all the women turned to face the mighty river, which was also in the direction of the horseshoe. Each woman and child seemed to feel the spirit of which Sunflower Woman had spoken. All was silent. There was no movement, even the children were motionless. Time seemed to stop for the group of broken-hearted Creek. Then the chilly wind began to blow. The women pulled their blankets close and just as a small child began to whimper, the eerie sound was heard. A sound the group associated as the prophesy of death and destruction, one they had hoped to never hear again. The cry of the owl. Many children began to cry loudly and some of the women began to keen once again. Sunflower Woman held up her hand to signal her people to silence. The owl's cry became louder as the winged creature flew into sight. Instead of perching as the horrified group anticipated, the owl continued its flight and soon vanished. The cry could be heard only faintly.

Sunflower Woman turned once again to face the group of trembling women and children. "My people, this is a good sign. The owl and his cry of death is gone. He has set us free and we must go now to begin our new life," Sunflower Woman said as the cheerful sound of a blue bird filled the air. Much to the relief of the White Stick warriors, the group then began to move, walking past what remained of the village of Tohopeka. The village which was intended to be a safe place had instead been a place of death and sorrow.

Little Flower, with her twin son and daughter turned to follow her mother. She too had experienced a strange feeling as they had approached the battle site. She had lost her father, her brother and her husband, Soaring Eagle, the leader of the Hillabee people. She still could not believe this had happened. She could not believe that she would never see her Eagle or know his love again. Little Flower suddenly felt the urge to stop, others bumping her as they began to move forward.

"My mother, I must remain here a little longer. I cannot leave. The spirit of Soaring Eagle is too strong," Little Flower said as she began to cry, again. "I will catch up soon."

Understanding the sorrow of her daughter, Sun Flower Woman nodded her approval. "Do not fall behind. Do not be left here alone. I fear the return of the white soldiers."

"Yes, my mother." Little Flower said as she moved from the path to allow the others to pass. "Please take the twins with you."

Little Flower watched as the other Creek women from Hillabee, Oakfuskee, Fish Pond and several other villages passed her by, each entrenched in their own grief. She stood silently, knowing she had a short time to remain before she too would need to go. She feared that she would never be allowed to return to her upriver home of Hillabee Town. The home where she was born and where she and Soaring Eagle had lived with so much happiness and love. Just as she began to walk forward, a soft wind began to blow. Little Flower stopped and turned again toward the direction of the battle site. She was engulfed by a strong feeling of not being alone. From far away, she heard faint sounds of someone in pain and anguish. Then even softer, Little Flower heard her name.

"Eagle, my Eagle," the excited young woman said as she began to run toward the battle site. "You, come back. You cannot go there." One of the White Stick Creek warriors shouted as he ran to stop the desperate woman, who even in her sorrow was very beautiful. "My husband, he still lives," Little Flower said as she tried to free herself from the warrior's grip. "I heard him call my name. I must go to him. I must help."

"No, I am sorry. No one lives. The soldiers made sure that none of the Red Sticks would live to see the setting sun," the warrior said remembering the scene from the day before that even now sickened him.

"I heard him. I know I heard him," Little Flower said as fresh tears fell from the dark pools of her eyes.

"He no longer lives," the warrior said again resisting the urge to take the beautiful woman in his arms to comfort her. "The spirit of the dead is still here. It was the spirit of your husband that you heard. You must let him go down the path of the Great Spirit. You must go now and join the others. The white soldiers are still near and they will harm you if they see you here alone. Go, you must go," the White Stick warrior said as he gently pushed the heartbroken woman down the path to join the other women and children.

Chapter Two

Little Flower, willing her tears to stop, begin quickly to walk down the path to reach her mother and children. As she brushed by an older woman from a village other than her own, the woman grabbed her arm.

"My grandmother," Little Flower said using the Creek term of respect for older women, "please forgive me. I need to reach my mother, Sun Flower Woman and in my haste I pushed you."

The old woman looked long into the tear-streaked face of the young woman. "I recognize you. You are the wife of Soaring Eagle, the leader of the Hillabee. My child, there is a strange look about you. What is wrong?" She asked, her wrinkled face filled with concern.

"Grandmother, "Little Flower said as tears begin to fall again. "I heard the voice of my husband and the White Stick told me that no one was left to speak."

"You have heard a voice from the spirit world. You must not be frightened. This is a good sign," the old woman said placing her frail hand on Little Flower's arm. "Your husband has spoken to you from the other side. It was his way to tell you that he is well now and for you to be strong."

"Grandmother, can this be? Why have others not heard voices?" Little Flower asked as a crowd gathered around them.

"Yes, my child. It is true. You and your husband must have had a special love for this to happen."

Word of Little Flower's experience traveled quickly through the line of women and children. Soon Sunflower Woman was by the side of the young woman. "My daughter, "the soft familiar voice was instantly calming. "What have you heard?"

Little Flower told her mother what had happened and what she had been told by both the warrior and the old woman.

"My mother, I do not believe the words of the warrior and do not think that I have heard the voice of Soaring Eagle from the spirit world. He is still of this world. I know he still lives," Little Flower quietly said as the group that had gathered parted to allow the White Stick warrior through.

Having inquired about the beautiful young woman, the warrior now knew who she was and her name. He understood her sorrow, but he also knew this group had to move on. They could not remain this close to the Horseshoe battle site. His orders where to get them to Tuckabatchee Town as soon as possible.

"Little Flower," the warrior said, "I am called Badger. I am from the town of Coweta. I do not intend to be cruel to you. You must listen to me. These women and children need to leave here now before the soldiers return," looking helpless he continued, "please go."

Having heard the words of the warrior now known as Badger, Sunflower woman took control of her group. "My child and my people, let us now go. There is nothing else that we can do here." With that the forlorn Creek families began to walk.

Chapter Three

The events that had occurred at the Horseshoe battle site had delayed the progress of the group, who were in fact captives. The cool winds of early spring had caused the old ones to again pull their blankets tighter and their walk became even slower. The sun began to drop in the western sky. They had made very little progress. Badger and the other White Stick Warriors realized camp would need to be made sooner than anticipated. A sufficient location for nearly fifty women, children and a few old men who were too old to fight, must now be found. Then there was the problem of food. The Coweta warriors were much more aware of the distance between the Horseshoe and Tuckabatchee Town than the white soldiers were. They knew the rationed supply of food would only last two days, at most, and the trip down river could take twice as long.

The captive group had walked in eerie silence since leaving the Horseshoe, each one trying to comprehend the horrors they had experienced. As the sun sank behind the line of red oak trees that bordered the river, the temperature dropped sharply. The younger children began to fret and the older women expressed their need to rest.

Sunflower Woman, in her place as leader and at the front of the group, had overheard the White Stick Warriors talking of the need to find a suitable camping area. Increasing her pace, the strong Creek woman called out so that she could be heard over the wind which had begun to howl through the trees.

"If we go to our left for a short distance, there is a flat area near a small steam where we can camp. A group of cedar trees there will protect us from the wind and we can catch fish to fill our stomachs." Sunflower woman said, hoping the warriors would listen to her.

Instead of disregarding her as Sunflower woman had feared, the warrior called Badger stopped and turned to face her and with a respectful tone said, "You are the one called Sun Flower Woman. How do you know of this place?"

"My husband," she paused, taking a deep breath, "and I once camped there." Taking the opportunity, she continued, "I, my people need to know if we are safe. Will the white soldiers harm us? Will we have food? How will we as families of Red Stick Warriors be treated when we get to Tuckabatchee and to your town on the river Chattahoochee?" Sun Flower Woman rapidly asked, seeing a slight glimmer of humor in the otherwise kind eyes of the warrior.

"Sunflower Woman," Badger said, becoming serious. "These are things you and your people should know and I will truthfully answer your questions. The soldiers are still in the area. I do not know if they will harm you again. I believe if we continue to move and none of you try to escape, you will be safe. There is not enough food. We will need to add to what we have from both the streams and what can be gathered from the forest." He paused not sure of what he would say next. "The treatment you will receive from Tuckabatchee and Coweta is not for me to know. Some of you will be accepted into families and some of you will become slaves. Some of you may be stoned or killed. As it was in your towns, the old women will decide your fate."

With the wisdom of many seasons and a renewed strength that even she did not understand, Sun Flower Woman calmly spoke to the kind warrior. "We will face one day at a time and we will do what is necessary to survive. For now, may I tell the others that we will camp by the stream near the cedar trees?"

Impressed by her strength and strong will, Badger answered, "Yes, tell your people we will camp where you have suggested. Tell them we will need to find additional food and," he paused, "Tell them to stay together and do not try to escape. I feel that we are being watched. If no time is wasted, we will be settled when the darkness of night comes. Lead the way."

Having nothing but their blankets, they were forced to resort to the ways of the grandmothers. By working together, the group of forlorn Creek created a sufficient make-shift camp. The children had been told to gather small sticks for fires and larger ones to make lean-tos. The White Stick Warriors refused to give the old injured men anything that could be used as a weapon, fearing they would attempt to escape. Instead, sticks were sharpened with stones to spear the fish. The women gathered the few hickory nuts that were scattered on the forest floor. Using none of the food rationed by the soldiers, as the White Stick Warriors had advised, a meager meal was shared by the exhausted group.

Chapter Four

As the last rays of the sun began to fade, the final cedar boughs were spread in front of the lean-tos. Badger had informed the group that once darkness fell they would need to stay in the camp, both for their own safety and to ensure that no one would try to escape.

"My mother," the tiny tired voice of a child was heard soon after the White Stick warrior had spoken. "My mother, I need water. My mouth is so dry. Please mother." The voice was that of Little Deer, the daughter of Little Flower.

Having no water bottles, the captives had to drink directly from the stream. Little Flower looked at Badger. "May I take my child down to the stream? She needs water. I will be quick."

The White Stick warrior frowned, "The child should have gotten water before the sunset."

Little Deer began to cough and tears ran down the little girl's dirt-streaked face. "Please." She cried.

Badger was moved by the child's plea and instantly was filled with a deep feeling of sorrow. He could not forget the images of the previous day and the horrendous battle where so many warriors had been brutally slain. Her father was surely one of them.

"Take the child and her brother," realizing that the wide-eyed boy sitting beside the little girl was her twin. He continued, "to the steam. Hurry. Darkness will cover the sky soon."

Little Flower nodded her head in appreciation also understanding the reason for quickness. "Come children. We must go now."

Little Flower took the hand of each child and ran toward the stream which was bordered by large evergreen bushes that completely blocked the view from camp. Both children dropped to their knees and used their hands to cup the cold water. Being thirsty as well, Little Flower bent to drink from the stream. As she started to drink, she was pulled roughly to her feet. Her mouth was quickly covered by a filthy hand that smelled of blood and her arms were painfully pulled behind her back. Little Flower watched in horror as her children were pushed to the ground by a dirty white man, his long greasy hair falling over his scar-marked face.

"Leave the young'uns," the smelly man griping Little Flower said. "We don't want them slowing us down. All we want is their pretty mama."

"Jas, you fool, if we don't take these brats with us, how long you think before they go hollering back to that bunch of savages," the scar-faced man said as he looked down at Little Deer and Red Fox.

"It don't matter what you do, kill'em for all I care. They is just dirty, rotten injuns. Like I said, I'm taking their mama," the man called Jas said as he began to run, pulling Little Flower with him.

Little Flower thinking quickly, looked at her children, hoping they would understand as she managed to wave her hand in the direction of the camp. Understanding completely, the children both jumped to their feet, moving just out of reach of Scarface and raced toward the camp. The men began running as they heard the children yelling for their grandmother.

"Jas, I told you this would be trouble," Scarface said, trying to overtake his partner. "But no, you just had to have this squaw."

"Shut up, I got her ain't I, and I intend to keep her, just run," Jas said as he threw Little Flower over his shoulder to quicken his pace.

"My grandmother, my grandmother," Little Deer screamed as the children reached the camp clearing.

"My children, what is wrong?" Where is your mother," Sun Flower Woman asked in alarm and fear?

"Two ugly, smelly white men took her," Red Fox yelled. "We have to go help. I know they plan to hurt her. One of them called her, his."

Little Deer noticed that the one called Badger was running toward them. She moved past her grandmother to meet him. "Please, go help my mother. The bad men will do mean things to her," the little girl said with a sense of maturity that surprised Badger.

"Little Deer, how many men, how were they dressed and did they go up or down the creek," Badger quickly asked as two other warriors ran to see what the commotion was about.

The little girl answered the questions with tears forming in her hug brown eyes. "Two men, one had a big scar on his face. They wore old, ragged clothes, not the blue of the soldiers and they went up the creek. One of them had my mother over his shoulder and was holding her mouth so she could not call for help. Please go help her." Little Deer fell into the arms of her grandmother as the three warriors began to run toward the stream.

Red Fox called out to them, "I am coming too. The men are not going to hurt my mother!"

Had the situation not been so grave, Badger would have laughed at the little boy, but instead he calmly said, "Red Fox, I need for you to stay here with you sister, we will bring your mother back.

Chapter Five

The two men, one still carrying Little Flower over his shoulder, made good time and managed to get a considerable distance from the stream. The terrified woman wisely remained still and calm, fearing her captors would kill her if she did not cooperate.

"Jas," Scarface said, gasping for air. "Jas, slow down and let me catch my breath. I think we are far enough away now. I still don't know why you had to have this squaw woman. We could be almost back to Georgie by now if we had left after we killed all them injuns yesterday."

"I done told you to shut up. And as sure is my name is Jasper Smith I intend to have me some fun with this pretty little thing. If you don't like it, you can just go on your way and I'll go mine."

Little Flower hearing what the disgusting, filthy man said and along with being joggled up and down, felt she was going to be sick. Using all her inner strength, she willed herself to concentrate on surviving and somehow finding a way to escape. Her thoughts turned to her husband, Soaring Eagle. She knew in her heart that he still lived, but also realized he could not help her.

As her captor slowed down to jump a small ravine, Little Flower caught a glimpse of movement through the trees. As she watched closely, she recognized Badger cautiously moving toward them.

"Ya know what ole Scarface, I think I do need to take me a little break, just as soon as we top that hill up yonder," Jas said, shifting his load to his other shoulder.

Hearing what was said, Badger and the two other warriors quickly circled around and hid behind a clump of bushes. Little Flower saw their maneuver and knew they would be waiting.

Jas roughly dropped Little Flower to the ground before sitting down on a log in front of the bushes. "Now girlie, you just sit yourself right there and don't you move, cause if'n you do, I might just have to hurt you and I sure don't want to hurt that pretty face," he threatened.

Little Flower caught the eye of Badger and watched in amazement as the warrior quickly rose and placed his knife on the throat of Jasper Smith. She saw the fine thread of blood begin to trickle down his chest. At the same time Scarface was taken to the ground by the other warriors. Badger pulled the wild-eyed man to his feet, his arms frantically waving in the air as he tried to free himself from the warrior's grip.

"You have plans to harm this woman," Badger asked as he pulled his knife tighter. "I think now it will be you who will be harmed," he whispered.

Scarface offered no resistance, fearing he too would feel a knife blade on his throat. "I had nothin' to do with this. I told him to leave her be. Jest let me go. I swear I will leave and never cause nobody no harm," the ugly man whimpered like a child.

Badger glanced at Little Flower, who sat perfectly still. She had a look of courage on her face that completely covered the fear she felt. "Where you hurt in any way," the White Stick warrior asked.

Little Flower shook her head, "No."

Badger slowly released the pressure of the knife. With one hand he grabbed the arms of the man and pulled them back. Jasper screamed in pain as one of the warriors tied his hands with a rope just as they had done to Scarface.

Badger removed his knife and roughly pushed the man to the ground. "Why do you think you can take this woman? She and her family have suffered much. You should die for what has already happened to her," the warrior scolded, as he clinched his knife again and raised it in the air.

"Please do not kill me. If you will let me live, I will leave this place and never return," Jas gasped as tears ran down his filthy face. I was not going to hurt her; I was jest, "Silence," Badger yelled, "I do not want to hear the words of a man who cries like a baby. See, the woman has more courage than you. I am not going to kill you. Not because you begged for your life but because the soldiers will come and harm these people again." Badger grabbed him, placing the knife once again to his throat. "If I ever see you again, you will die. Now go from my sight," he said as he shoved him in the direction of the path.

Both men, with their hands still tied, stumbling, began to run. Scarface turned and nodded his head in appreciation. He began yelling at the man in front of him, "Jas, you nearly got us killed this time. When we get back home, I am going to tell your woman what you done and I spect she'll kill you herself."

Jasper did not answer as tears still ran down his face, mingling with the blood from his throat.

Badger placed his knife back in his belt and looked at Little Flower. He again resisted the urge to take her in his arms. He knew she was terrified but had remained calm in order to survive. As he took her hand and lifted her to her feet he gently said, "Now we will go. I promised your son I would bring you back."

"Thank you," Little Flower said, too shaken to say more. As the moon rose over the trees, the beautiful young woman and the warriors made their way back to camp.

Chapter Six

Only the children and the very old slept as the wind whistled through the trees. Many had no blankets and the ground was damp and cold. The others sat huddled around the fires taking turns adding sticks and branches. The night sounds, the distant yelping of the coyotes, the raucous raccoons and the sad call of the hoot owls made the already nervous Creek women even more edgy.

The white stick warriors stood guard, more for their protection than any escape. They knew that a few of the white soldiers still remained in the area and there was always the possibility that some of the rouge white men were still around. Badger would like to have killed the disgusting men who had taken Little Flower, but realized there would have been retaliation. He and the other warriors were tired of the fighting and bloodshed. They only wanted to go home.

"Badger," one of them asked as he stirred the fire nearest to them. "How long do you think it will take us to get these people to Tuckabatchee? Will we take any of them on to the Chattahoochee with us?"

Badger smiled, the firelight splashing on his strong face. "At the pace we are making, many suns. I hope to move faster with the new day. We have had much delay. I need to sleep now," he said as he rolled himself into a tight ball near the fire. The sleep of Badger was fitful as he dreamed of the two white men, one with an ugly scar and the other grinning evilly as he threw Little Flower to the ground.

Chapter Seven

Badger had his charges ready to move by the time pink tints streaked in the eastern sky. He called for the group to move in closer as he had important words to say to them. "We are in day two of our journey to Tuckabatchee Town," he paused, frowning. "We should be almost half way there and we have only just begun. On this day, we will walk far before we stop. We will give each of you some parched corn now and again when the sun is high in the sky. For now, that is all the food. Our pace will be swift. Do not fall behind. When dark of the night comes, we must be at the village of Okfuskee. Let us go now," he instructed.

The wretched group of Creek began to walk with Sunflower Woman again taking the lead. Little Flower had spoken very little, her experience of the evening before had frightened her more than she realized and the feeling that her husband still lived and needed help was heavy on her heart. She reached for the hands of her children and joined her mother at the front of the line.

Looking at the grief-stricken face of her daughter, Sunflower Woman herself, fighting back tears, began to sing an ancient song of the grandmothers. Suddenly others joined in, filling the air with a soft melody of pain and sorrow. The women continued to sing as they walked, the strong spirit of the grandmothers filling their heart.

Little Flower had dropped the hands of her son and daughter. She sang with the other women; a peace began to wash over her. After walking for a while, she realized that her children were no longer by her side. Startled she turned to look for them as she called their names. When Little Flower received no answer, she began to run back through the line of women, hoping the children had stopped along the way with their friends.

"Have you seen my children, Little Deer and Red Fox," the anxious woman asked as she passed by each family. Nearing the end of the line, an older woman that Little Flower was unacquainted with answered her.

"Yes, I saw a little boy and little girl running back the way we came. I asked where they were going and they told me they were going to find their father."

Little Flower's heart sank as she continued running back up the path. Badger was bringing up the rear when he saw the woman running toward him.

"Little Flower," the White Stick Warrior shouted. "Where are you going? I said we have to move quickly and you are wasting time."

"My children," Little Flower said, stopping to catch her breath. "They have gone back. I must go find them."

"Why have they gone back? I did not see them," Badger said frowning as he grabbed her arm.

"To look for their father," Little Flower said, pulling away from him.

"I told you that Soaring Eagle no longer lives. What do they expect to find?" Badger angrily asked. "Woman, you and your children have caused much trouble. The group will continue to move. I will go back for them," he scolded as he walked away.

"I am going with you. I do not intend to move forward without them," Little Flower said with tears again filling her eyes.

Badger turned to look at the beautiful woman, feeling a little tug in his heart. "Come, we must hurry, they cannot have gone far. I hope they remained near the path. If they did not, they will be harder to locate."

Badger and Little Flower had not walked far before they saw the children running up the path in front of them.

"Red Fox, Little Deer, stop now," Badger yelled. The children stopped, realizing by the sound of the warrior's voice that they were in trouble.

Little Flower ran to her children and hugged them both. "What is the reason for this? You know we have far to go."

"My mother", Red Fox said, "We heard you say our father still lives. We only wanted to go to him."

"Yes, mother," Little Deer said as she began to cry. "He needs our help. We are sorry mother to cause trouble. We should have asked you to come with us."

Badger stood watching the tender scene before him, his anger diminished as the little girl looked up at him crying, "Please help us look for our father."

Badger looked at Little Flower and then back to the children, each awaiting his answer. "I am sorry. Your father does not live. I have the responsibility to get all of your people to Tuckabatchee Town and on to Coweta." Seeing the disappointment in their face, he continued, "Once I do that, I will return to look for your father. If I find him," pausing again, not wanting to lie to them, "I will return him to you. Now, we must go catch up with the others." Badger picked up the little boy and indicated for Little Flower to carry her daughter. "Promise me you will not cause any more trouble."

Badger was surprised at the distance the group had traveled when he, Little Flower and the children caught up. They continued their pace, stopping only briefly when the sun was over head. He was also amazed at the determination to survive these women seemed to have. All of them had suffered great loss and knew not what the future for them would be. When the brief time of rest was over, Badger addressed the group. All of them, even the children, listened attentively. "I think," he paused with a slight smile, "that if we make good time, we can reach Oakfuskee before the sun no longer shines, that is, if we do not have more delays," he finished, looking at Red Fox and Little Deer who tried to hide behind their mother and grandmother. "One more thing before we resume our journey. I do not know what we will find. Okfuskee may have suffered the fate as other towns. There may be nothing left. I have some food. It may be the last we will have until we arrive at Tuckabatchee Town."

The women seemed to take a deep breath, but said nothing and once again resumed their march. The few old men began talking among themselves, but they too, soon became silent. There was nothing they could do.

Chapter Eight

Badger had sent two of the warriors ahead to see if Oakfuskee Town remained intact. As he had told the group, he did not know what to expect. He had not been down the path since the battle at the Horseshoe had occurred, a battle that he wished he had not been a part.

His people, living on the Chattahoochee had not experienced the problems created by the white man as the Upper Creek had at their homes along the Tallapoosa and Coosa Rivers. The Coweta had freely excepted more of the white ways and were not forced to fight with the white soldiers. In fact, his town of Coweta lived in perfect harmony with their white neighbors.

Badger had not realized when he and his friends volunteered to accompany Chief McIntosh to the Upper Creek territory that they would be involved in such horrible actions.

They had fought in minor battles against the Red Stick warriors and even killed one or two. They had never intended to participate in a battle where their opponents were outnumbered three to one and had few weapons with which to fight. The Red Stick warriors were only trying to defend themselves and their families. Badger knew if he could change what had happened, he would, but he could not, and instead found himself in charge of homeless women and children with no husbands and fathers, and he was responsible for taking them to face, he knew not what.

Badger was deep in thought over the events of the past few days and did not realize how far his group had walked until he recognized a bend in the path that led back toward the Tallapoosa. The path they had traveled from the Horseshoe had veered away from the river and was the shortest route to Tuckabatchee Town. He was relieved that they would reach Okfuskee before darkness fell. This is good, he thought to himself, these people deserve to rest and have food other than dry corn. He hoped the town had not been destroyed. Possibly, there would be more food available. He was hungry himself and knew the women and children were ravished. He continued to be amazed by the stamina they had shown.

His thoughts were interrupted by the return of the two warriors he had sent ahead. He could tell by the serious expressions on their faces that the report would not be good. "My brothers, what news do you have for me," Badger asked as the warriors slowed to catch their breath.

"Badger," the older of the two said, "The village is partially burned. There seems to have been a struggle of some sort and no people are anywhere to be found."

"That is what I feared. Do you think that any food remains there," Badger asked as some of the women had stopped to hear the report of the warriors.

"It is possible. It looks like everyone, both attackers and the village people left quickly. I could not tell if they left together," the warrior said, looking at the desolate women.

"We will see what remains soon," Badger said, turning back to the two warriors. "Return to the village ahead of us. Watch for any signs of the soldiers or those disgusting men from Georgia. Nothing else is going to happen to these people while they are under my protection."

Chapter Nine

The sun was low in the sky when the exhausted group reached the outskirts of the village of Oakfuskee. The scouts who had been sent ahead found no soldiers, but reported that several dead Creek remained in one of the unburned huti.

Badger told the women and children to prepare to camp, giving them the bundles of corn and meat he had brought with him. He wanted to check on the condition of the village himself.

Walking around the partially destroyed village, he saw again the horrendous destruction the white people could do. Most of the huti were burned and he saw the slain warriors lying in various grotesque positions of death. He quickly had his warriors remove them from sight before the women saw them. The keening began once again as the women and children wondered around the remains of the village.

"Will this ever end," one old women cried out. "How can these white people continue to kill and kill more? What do they want from us?" She finished with tears streaming down her wrinkled face. Others hearing the old woman began to cry as well, each recounting their own sorrows.

Seeing that her people were again sinking to a low place in spirit, Sunflower Woman rushed forward and admonished, "Grandmothers, do not go down the sad path. Come, help me. Let us look for more food and make fires. We should eat and rest so that we may travel again on the new day. We still have far to go to reach Tuckabatchee Town." Turning to face the group who had gathered around, Sunflower Woman continued, "Please, each of you remember that we are women of the Creek. We are of the Clan of the Bear, the Bird, the Potato, and the mighty Wind. We are strong. We have the spirit of many Hillabee grandmothers flowing in us and we will survive. We will live so that our children and their children can live. The Creek people will not perish," Sunflower Woman finished as she herself wiped a tear from her eye.

The women were able to find additional dried corn and beans stored in one of the unburned huti. This, along with the small amount of food given to the Creek warrior by the white soldiers would provide an ample meal.

Using some of the iron pots and unbroken clay bowls that had been left behind by the Okfuskee people, the women prepared hot stew for the weary travelers. The meal seemed to stabilize the group and settle their frayed nerves.

Badger noticed that preparations for the night were done quickly and smoothly. He was reluctant to speak to his charges for fear of upsetting them, but he knew that he had to tell them of the plans for the upcoming day. A full moon shown over the horizon as he began to speak, "Brother moon is big on this night and that is good. We will use his light to see as we begin the last part of our journey before the new day. We will not sleep again until we reach Tuckabatchee Town," he said noticing, as he had expected, the fear and uncertainty that reappeared on the faces of the older women.

As she had done previously, Sunflower Woman stepped forward, the strength and confidence of the woman showing on her still beautiful face, "My people need to know what happened to the Oakfuskee families who made their homes here. Where are they? Are they being taken to Tuckabatchee Town too and," she paused to catch her breath aware that Badger was amused by her rapid-fire questions, "We have asked this before. How will we, the families of Red Stick warriors, be treated by the Tuckabatchee people?" Badger, fully aware of the earnestness and sincerity of the woman's questions could not help but smile as he exclaimed, "Woman, the Red Stick warriors needed you as their leader," quickly sobering he tried to answer Sun Flower Woman who stood glaring at him. "I do not know what happened to the Oakfuskee people. The men," Badger stopped not wanting to speak the hurtful words of truth, "were at the Horseshoe and women and children like you are being taken to other places and other towns. They may not be treated as kindly as you. As far as your treatment at Tuckabatchee Town," he shook his head again, "I tell you that I do not know. It may be that some of you will continue with me to Coweta Town. Now, I wish for you to sleep, we will begin while Brother Moon is still shining high in the sky." As Badger finished, he looked out at the group, his eyes resting on Little Flower and her children.

Chapter Ten

Succumbing to the fatigue that washed over them, the Creek women and children quickly fell into a deep sleep. Having found blankets left behind by the Oakfuskee people, they were warm and comfortable. The few old men of the group had, to their delight, found a small amount of tobacco and sat around the fire smoking and talking of their fate. Taking a long draw from his pipe, one of the older men who had been only slightly wounded, finally said, "I am sure we will be killed, they will have no use for us."

Another, nursing his arm which still contained a small musket ball added, "I agree and I for one do not intend for that to happen to me."

"What are your plans then," yet another of the more mature and wiser asked. "Tell us what you are thinking?"

"I plan to leave this camp while the moon shines brightly. The man called Badger and his little band of warriors will need to sleep. When they do, I will go," he replied with obvious contemp.

You will be shot if you are caught trying to escape," the man holding the pipe answered.

"Shot now or killed later. I will take my chances. I am a Red Stick Warrior and I do know how to fight and defend myself," the injured man replied.

The men sat in silence, each thinking of what had been said. Suddenly, another voiced his opinion. "I too will leave. We need to have a plan. Where shall we go?"

"I think, back up river past the Horseshoe. I know of a bluff shelter that extends far back into the hill and forms a cave. We can hide there until the white soldiers leave the area," the warrior said, looking at his wound. "Then one of you can cut this lead ball from my arm," he exclaimed, grimacing in pain.

In only a short time plans had been made and each one of the old Red Stick Warriors, regaining their fighting spirit, said that he would go.

"What of the women and children," one of the men asked. "Will they be harmed?"

"This Badger seems to be fair. I think he will see to it, if possible, that they will be safe," the oldest of the group said. "And I know he will look after the wife of Soaring Eagle."

"Soaring Eagle will return from the spirit world if he looks after her too well," another answered with a smile.

The old warriors planned to feign sleep, watching for the opportunity to escape. The moon continued to shine brightly. The sounds of the wild, the yelping of the coyote and the call of the hoot owl filled the night air. As the moon reached its highest point in the sky, the warrior standing watch over the group began to nod, slumping over against a tree near him. This was the chance for which they had waited. The old warriors, one by one, quickly slipped out of the make-shift camp. No one saw them leave except Sun Flower Woman. She prayed to the Giver of Breath that they could escape and be safe. She knew as they did, if they were caught they would be shot and if they continued with the group, they would likely be killed.

Chapter Eleven

The group of Creek were aroused from their deep sleep, as Brother Moon continued to shine brightly over the camp. Badger immediately noticed that the men were no longer there. With obvious anger in his voice, he demanded, "Which of you were standing guard last? Who let the men, the Red Stick Warriors escape?" Looking from warrior to warrior, his coal black eyes sparkled in the moonlight.

"Badger," a young warrior who had only recently obtained his warrior name, stepped forward. "Badger, I was the one who could not keep the sleep away. I allowed the Red Stick Warriors to escape." The young warrior did not ask for any pardon and had honestly admitted his guilt.

Badger liked to see this maturity in such a young warrior and his anger began to subside.

"I should send you after them. They could not have gotten far," Badger paused, "but you would need to shoot them if you found them. There is no point. They would be put to death in Tuckabatchee anyway. If I were one of them, I also would have escaped. The path may still have soldiers and ugly white men roaming around and if they are found, they will still die. If the old Red Stick Warriors can survive, then I say that is good. I am tired of death and destruction. I am ready to go home," Badger declared as he looked over his charges and predicted, "We will soon begin and we will see Tuchabatchee Town before Brother Moon shows his face when the day is finished.

Chapter Twelve

The Red Stick families and the white peace warriors walked at a steady pace, making good time, and covering a great distance, stopping only when the group reached the stream of the Turtle Rattler.

To his dismay, Badger saw the red water churning over the rocks at precisely the point of crossing. Upstream rains had caused the normally small stream to become, instead, a small river which would be impossible for the women and children to safely ford. With a sound of exasperation, the White Stick Warrior turned to the women. "We will not be able to cross here and we will be delayed," he paused, "once more."

He was not surprised when Sunflower Woman stepped forward. "We need to rest and have food. It is possible that in that time the waters will run down enough so that we may cross," She said, again showing the wisdom of having seen many seasons. Turning to face the women, she calmly asked them to bring all food they had saved and to forage for anything else that could be eaten.

The wise old woman had been correct. After the meal was finished and the time of rest completed, Badger noticed that indeed the water flow had diminished greatly. "Sunflower Woman, how did you know the stream would return to nearly normal so quickly," the kindly White Stick Warrior asked as he looked up and down the stream for the best place to cross.

"I have seen many suns. My people are now ready to continue our journey," Sunflower Woman said as she beckoned the others to prepare to move. "The crossing may still be treacherous. I think it best for us to cross just upstream on the natural bridge of rocks. Caution should be used as the rocks will be slippery.

Continuing to be amazed and a little embarrassed, Badger followed Sunflower Woman's lead. He still hoped to reach

Tuckabatchee Town before Brother Moon showed his light.

Following the warriors, the women and children safely maneuvered the stream of Turtle Rattlers, leaving only Sunflower Woman, Little Flower, and the twins along with Badger to cross over. Instead of becoming dryer, the large stones became wet and slick from the mud that had been splashed on them as the others had crossed. Sunflower Woman and her grandson had just taken the final step off the rocks when the sound of a large splash vibrated in the air.

Turning quickly, Sunflower Woman saw the dark head of her granddaughter sink into the muddy water. At the same time the large frame of Badger dove in for her, his strong arms securing the tiny little girl, pulling her to the surface. Both warrior and child were gasping for air, the child choking on the muddy water. Little Flower took her daughter from Badger, holding her close as tears streamed down her face. Memories returned of a similar event that happened long, long ago when her beloved Soaring Eagle had saved her too from certain death.

Not completely understanding the emotion shown by Little Flower, Badger stood shaking the water from his body as he looked upon the mother and child, assuring Little Flower, "Your daughter is unharmed." Appearing exasperated, he continued, "The others must go now if they are to reach Tuckabatchee Town this day. We will build a fire and dry the child's clothing," he paused, "and mine, then we will resume our journey."

"Thank you," Little Flower said as she wiped the tears from her face, "once again."

Badger smiled slightly at the beautiful woman, trying to quell the forbidden emotions that he felt. This woman had just lost her husband and it was wrong to have any feelings for her other than concern and the obligation to get her and the other women and children to Tuckabatchee and Coweta.

Chapter Thirteen

Badger gave instructions for the others to move forward on what he hoped was the last part of their journey. He knew their destination could be reached barring any further delays. He and Little Flower and her daughter could catch up quickly. He had just turned to build the fire when he heard the voice of Red Fox calling from across the creek. "I will stay with my mother and sister," the boy said as he began to come back the way he had crossed only minutes before.

"I think it best that you go on with your grandmother," Badger called back to the child.

"My mother and my sister need my protection and I can help protect them," Red Fox yelled as he safely stepped from the last rock to the bank.

"Let the child remain. I will go with my people and help to keep them moving. You will catch up before we have gone far," Sun Flower Woman said as she began to walk.

Badger looked at Red Fox and began to laugh. "I have never seen children like the two of you. It is important that you look after your mother and your sister, even if it puts you in danger."

"Yes, it is. I promised my father that I would take care of them," the child said as he ran to stand by the side of his mother. "And you are a White Stick Warrior. You are kind to us, but you came to fight our people."

Suddenly sobering, with a feeling of regret washing over him, Badger stooped to rekindle the fire used earlier. Little Deer wrapped herself in a blanket as her mother placed the child's skirt and shirt on forked sticks near the fire. Badger also removed his shirt and did the same. Little Flower and her son took advantage of the opportunity to rest before resuming the remainder of their journey. Nothing was said as the warrior and the little family sat and gazed at the fire as if willing the warmth to heal their pain. The sweet voice of Little Deer broke the awkward silence as she pulled the blanket closer.

"Why did you come to our town to fight with our warriors? Why did you kill our people and why do we have to go to this Tuckabatchee Town? Are you called a White Stick Warrior because you like the white people more than the Creek people? Are you not a Creek too?" She asked, as tiny tears rolled down the little girl's cheeks, her tear-filled eyes searching the face of the White Stick Warrior.

Badger looked at Little Deer and her brother before his eyes locked with those of Little Flower. He could feel the lump forming in his throat. "I," he paused, "I did not realize so many would not live to see the new day. I did not know villages would be burned and families would be scattered. I did not know the white leaders talked with such forked tongues. I am Creek just as you are and," he paused again as his voice broke, "I am sorry to have been involved," Badger said, tuning away, pretending to adjust his shirt.

Little Flower pulled her children near her. Her sorrow deep and raw, she began again to sing one of the ancient songs of the grandmothers. As she sang, sunlight broke through the clouds and the sweet song of a bluebird calling his mate echoed through the trees.

"The clothes of Little Deer are nearly dry. I think we should move on. My mother will be watching for us," Little Flower said as she helped her child dress.

Badger had composed himself and pulled his hunting shirt over his head. He knew that he wanted this little family to be safe and happy again and he also knew he wanted to help. He realized he, the wise warrior from Coweta Town, was falling in love not only with the intelligent little children, but also with their mother. No, no, he thought to himself, this is not good.

"Yes, let us move. We have not yet lost much time. We can soon join the others," Badger said as he took Little Deer in his arms. "I do not wish for another swim today. Little Flower hold onto your son as we cross the creek."

Badger, Little Flower, and the children walked at a fast pace and soon saw the other Creek women and children. Nothing else had been said about the old warriors who had escaped and he hoped they were safe. He also assumed that Sun Flower Woman saw them leave and may have assisted them in some way or another. That was good too. Badger prayed to the Great Spirit that these people would be safe at Tuckabatchee Town and more importantly that they would be accepted.

Encountering no more delays, the group continued their journey. As the last rays of the sun slid beneath the horizon, the vast town of Tuckabatchee came into view.

****

Chapter Fourteen

The old Red Stick Warriors had moved quietly and quickly away from the make-shift camp. They were elated that the White Sticks had not followed and attempted to force them to go back. They did not realize that Badger had made the decision to let them go and hoped they would make it to where ever they intended to go.

The warriors had walked nonstop for the remainder of the night and the morning sun was high in the sky before the dreadful sight of the Horseshoe battle came into view. They were not prepared for what they saw. The birds of death still circled, more of them diving to the earth. The smell forced the warriors to cover their nose and mouth. Taking in the scene before them, Wolf Fella, the self-appointed leader of the group, began to chant. Using some of the same words the women used in their songs, the old warrior asked for strength from the Great Spirit. When he finished, Wolf Fella turned and spoke to his followers. "My Brothers, I have lived to see many suns. I have suffered much sadness. On this day, I now feel the pain and sorrow of all Creek warriors since before time of our grandfathers. I not know what to do or where we will go. We must bury as many of these brave warriors as we can," Wolf Fella lamented, his voice breaking. Tears streamed down his dirty, wrinkled face as he looked at the scene of lifeless bodies before him. "Do any of our warriors still live? Oh, Great Spirit, give our people strength to carry on, so that these valiant men will not have died in vain. Our people must survive. We will take bodies to that clump of trees and dig one big grave and cover it with rocks. Death birds and scavenger animals cannot disturb then. It look's like some dead warriors were pulled away and thrown into river by white soldiers. Let us begin now with this most unpleasant task," Wolf Fella said as he gathered his long gray hair and securely tied it back with a worn leather thong.

The old warriors had moved several of their slain comrades, gasping with horror in the recognition of many. Wolf Fella stopped as he heard a soft moan. "Did you hear that," he asked, not sure himself of what he had heard.

"Yes, yes, I did hear what sounded like a man," One of the warriors said as he looked around for any sign of movement.

"Someone still lives!" Another exclaimed, "Let us find him and try to help."

Then moaning became louder as if the injured person realized that help was near.

"There he is," Wolf Fella shouted as he quickly ran to the side of a man, his face covered with dried blood.

"Can you tell who he is," One of the warriors asked as Wolf Fella kneeled over the victim.

"No, he is in terrible mess and very badly injured. He has deep gash on head and looks like he was stabbed in stomach," Wolf Fella said as he examined the injuries.

"Can he be moved?" Another old warrior asked, peering over the shoulder of Wolf Fella.

"One of you find something to hold water. If we can clean him up, we can determine if he can be moved to a safe place. The rest of you carry dead to grave site. I try to comfort him and watch for any soldiers that still be lurking around. We need to hurry. We are not safe here in the open like this," Wolf Fella said as he covered the unknown warrior with a worn blanket he had found on the ground.

The warrior continued to moan in pain, moving in and out of conscientious. The old warrior quickly returned with water, having found a canteen that had been dropped by a soldier. Tearing cloth from his shirt, and soaking it with water, Wolf Fella gently washed the blood from the face of the warrior. As the cold water covered his face, the injured man slowly opened his eyes.

"Can you tell us who you are," Wolf Fella softly asked as he slowly lifted the man's head, offering him water from the canteen.

Allowing a trickle of the water to run down his throat, the warrior whispered, "Soaring Eagle." Closing his eyes in pain, he again said his name, "Soaring Ea-gle, I am Soaring Eagle of Hillabee."

****

Chapter Fifteen

"My mother, the Oakfuskee is so big here. How will we cross over," Red Fox asked as the group of women and children stood in awe of both the magnificent river and the sprawling town on the other side.

His mother shook her head. "I do not know. The river is much larger here. I think Badger will have the answer," Little Flower said, having to shout to be heard over the sound of the rapidly moving water.

"Look," the little boy shouted, pointing to a woven, hemp bridge swinging over the water. "Oh, I know I will be afraid to do this." Assuming they would need to cross the river on the bridge, the women began to back away from the water's edge.

"I will not be afraid," Little Deer exclaimed, "and I will be first."

Badger laughed at the child, remembering the swim they had taken earlier in the day. "None of us will cross over on the bridge. That is for strong warriors. One of my strong warriors has already crossed and will bring back large canoes." Looking at the sinking sun, Badger frowned. "I had hoped to be safely in Tuckabatchee Town before darkness covered the sky. We will need to move swiftly. Here they come now. Please use caution when getting in and out of the canoes. This is not Turtle Rattler Creek we are crossing this time," Badger warned.

"Badger," Sunflower woman called out as the first of three large canoes slid into the river bank. "My people need to be reassured. You must have had contact with the Tuckabatchee people. Will we be treated kindly or …."

"Sunflower Woman, my friend, do not concern yourself with your treatment. The people of Tuckabatchee will welcome you," Badger said as he lifted Little Deer into the canoe. "Come, while we still have light to see."

Safely getting the Creek women and children across the swift water of the Tallapoosa was the simplest task Badger had experienced with the people he now considered as his friends. There had been no problems and even Little Deer had managed the crossing without getting wet.

A large crowd of curious Tuckabatchee people had gathered to watch as the Red Stick families were helped from the canoes by the warriors who had guided them from the Horseshoe. While not openly hostile, many of the Tuckabatchee did not appear overly friendly, either. Badger, observing this reaction from the Tuckabatchee, quickly herded his charges up the path toward the shining fire lights of the village. He had promised they would be well treated. He wondered now if he had been wrong.

Some of the younger children, fearing the sight of so many unfamiliar faces, began to softly cry. Their mothers silenced them, but they too were uncomfortable. The refugee Creek women and children entered the square ground of Tuckabatchee and suddenly many more residents surrounded them. Some of the warriors carried their guns as if expecting a battle to ensue. Badger was not sure what would happen next. He saw no sign of any official leader to quell the crowd if necessary. Deciding to defuse problems before any could arise, he stepped forward.

"I am Badger of Coweta Town on the Chattahoochee. These woman and children made their homes on the upper regions of the Tallapoosa. I was told to bring them here and that you would make them welcome. They have walked far and they are hungry and tired," Badger said, still scanning the crowd in search of someone in control. Where was Chief Big Warrior? He had been told to turn these people over to him and that they would be safe. This was not a good situation. Badger would not allow any of these women and children to be harmed in anyway.

"They are the women and children of the Red Stick Warriors. The warriors who have caused us much trouble. Why should we help them? They should go to one of the Red Stick towns if they are hungry," a young warrior clad in the shirt of a white man yelled.

Badger recognized her voice immediately and was not surprised when Sunflower Woman stepped forward and began to speak. "I am Sunflower Woman of the Hillabee. Yes, we are the families of Red Stick Warriors, warriors who no longer live. Each of us have lost a husband, a father, a son, or brother. We have no village and there are no other Red Stick villages left for us to go," the beautiful older woman paused, wiping the tears from her face. "If you do not wish for us to stay, we will go with Badger to his town on the Chattahoochee. Please give us food, if only for the children."

The murmuring crowd suddenly became silent, their eyes focused on the forlorn group before them. A small voice of a Tuckabatchee woman slowly became louder. "My brother is a Red Stick. He left here to go to the Horseshoe. I do not know if he lives. My family will help," looking around at others standing near her, she continued, "These people are Creek just as we are. It does not matter that some of us choose the white way and others wish to live as the grandmothers. It is the Creek way to help anyone who is in need. These people have no village and no warriors to provide food. It is our responsibility to help them."

The crowd parted as a tall, large framed warrior, his face marked with strange white spots, entered the square ground. "That is true. We will give them food and shelter for tonight," the large man said as he turned to face Badger and the group of frightened women and children. "I am Big Warrior, Civil Chief of Tuckabatchee. I was told to expect you and these people of the Red Stick. I did not know their number would be so great," the large man said, the firelight shining on his face, making him appear sinister and evil to the children.

"Big Warrior, I am Badger of the Coweta. Yes, General McIntosh told me to bring these surviving families of the Red Stick Warriors here before continuing to the Chattahoochee," Badger said with more courage than he felt. He was facing Chief Big Warrior and he was a little intimidated by the big

Spirit of the Red Stick Women

man, who was not as friendly and courteous as he had hoped and was told he would be. "Their total number is forty," Badger paused, thinking it best not to admit to the Chief that six old warriors had escaped. "General McIntosh advised me to ask if any of these people would be allowed to stay in Tuckabatchee Town, keeping families together. If this is not suitable for you and your people, I will take all of them to Coweta," where they will be welcome, Badger thought to himself.

Realizing that his words had been harsh, the big man looked again at the women and children. "Any who have clan or family members here may stay," pausing as if he was not being completely honest, he continued, "And anyone else who wishes will be welcome at Tuchabatchee. That will be determined with the new sun", he said as he looked to his assistants standing beside him, "please have the women prepare food and find shelter for these people from the upper Tallapoosa towns." As he began to walk away, he turned and looked at Badger and added, "you and your warriors are welcome to join us. We would like a first-hand report about what happened at the Horseshoe."

Chapter Sixteen

The next day dawned beautiful and clear as the sun's gentle rays appeared over the east bank of the Tallapoosa. The roar of the upriver falls could be distinctively heard, sounding much closer than they were. The previous night, the women and children of the upper Tallapoosa towns had all been given food and rested well, giving in to the fatigue that had overwhelmed them.

Badger had made the decision to continue to the Chattahoochee as soon as it was decided which families would stay at Tuckabatchee Town and which would go with him. A few of the group had indicated that they had clan members here and one or two had closer family members as well.

Badger had talked with the Tuckabatchee headmen and smoked their tobacco until late in the night. He told them of the horrors that had taken place at the Horseshoe and how he regretted his part in the slaughter. Many of the Tuckabatchee warriors had laughed at his remark and had ridiculed him, saying the was weak like a woman. These men had not been at the Horseshoe and the few Tuckabatchee warriors who had been there had not yet returned. Badger did not know that they were still burning and looting Red Stick towns along the river

The bustling town soon came to life as the morning meal was prepared for both the Tuckabatchee people and the Horseshoe refugees. Badger noticed that some of them had already parred off with resident families, but most stood off to the side, uncomfortably waiting to be told what they should do. Among those were Sunflower Woman, Little Flower, and her children.

As Badger walked by them he smiled, overhearing Little Deer softly talking to her mother, "My mother, I do not think we should stay here. These Tuckabatchee people do not like us.

Spirit of the Red Stick Women

The other children called me a Red Stick hostile. Mother, what is a hostile?" Before Little Flower could answer her daughter, the child continued, "I told them that I was a Red Stick and I am proud and that I did not like their town. Mother, can we go to the other town on the River of Flowered Rocks?"

Badger did not hear Little Flower as she sadly answered her daughter, "I do not know, Little Deer. We will do what is decided for us. I wish to go back to Hillabee Town. I wish to go back home and find your father."

Big Warrior had left before sunrise to attend business at one of the other towns in the Creek Nation. He had again extended the invitation for any who wished to stay in Tuckabatchee Town. Realizing that most of the Tuckabatchee did not want the Horseshoe refugees to remain, all but four women and their five children decided to move on.

Before the sun had topped the trees, Badger had his charges back across the Tallapoosa and well on their way to the Chattahoochee. The distance to Coweta Town was further than the trip from the Horseshoe, but the weather was better and he planned to use the horse path for part of the journey, making camp only once.

It was possible they would encounter others on the path. He knew that many undesirable men traveled the path and he and his warriors would need to use caution. One of the warriors had already been sent ahead to Coweta Town so that preparations could be made for the Horseshoe refugees. These were his people now and he would not allow them to be harmed or mistreated in any way. He was confident that the Coweta would welcome them to their town.

Chapter Seventeen

Carefully, maneuvering their way across the many pools of standing water that covered the horse path, the group at last reached a place to rest. Badger was amazed at these people who had lost so much and who had been treated somewhat unkindly by the Tuckabatchee people. None of them complained and even the children continued their solemn journey without whining.

Badger hoped to be out of this dismal place, known as Calebee Swamp before darkness covered the sky. "We will rest here and eat. Soon we will be back on our way. Are all of you ready to move on rapidly," the kindly White Stick Warrior asked as he looked at the women and children, his eyes, as always resting on Little Flower and her family. "We do not need to be in this place when the sun no longer shines," Badger added.

"We are ready to move again when we are told," Sunflower Woman answered for the group. "How many suns until we will reach the town that is your home," she questioned.

"If we have no trouble, we will sleep on the banks of the Chattahoochee before the sun rises for the second time," Badger paused, again looking over his charges of forlorn people. "Thank you, all of you for the valiant effort you are showing. I realize this is a difficult time. I promise you safety and comfort in your new home."

After a brief rest and parched corn had satisfied their hunger, the group began walking once more. They had not traveled far before Badger heard his name called from the rear of the group. He had told two of his warriors to lag behind, making sure they would not be surprised by some ruffian travelers on the path.

Badger paused as the warriors quickly ran to his side, both gasping for breath. "Is there a sign of trouble," he asked, looking back down the long line of women and children. "Did you see anyone coming up the path."

"Yes, we need to get these people away from the path and hide them in the swamp. A group of ten or twelve filthy white men are not far behind us," one of the warriors informed.

The other quickly added, "They act as if they have consumed much firewater. They are making loud noises and I think these people will be in danger. We need to move fast, they will be here very soon."

Badger wasted no time in moving his people from the path. Fortunately, there was a small opening, possibly a trail made by deer, which led deeper into the swamp. The women and children followed Badger's instructions and they were soon hidden from sight.

Chapter Eighteen

Badger left Sunflower Woman in charge of the now horrified group, telling her to keep everyone silent and to remain hidden until he returned for them. He made his way back to the path and sat down by his warriors. He heard the rowdy bunch of men coming before he saw them. "I will talk to these pathetic men and hopefully they will move on without causing any trouble," Badger paused just as the white men saw him and his warriors, "Be ready to defend yourself if necessary."

Wiping tobacco juice from his mouth with a filthy hand, the leading man proclaimed loudly, "Well, look what we done found, some ah them injuns."

An equally disgusting man chimed in saying, "I guess we didn't kill all of them after all. What da you say boys, wanta kill us some more?"

Slowly rising while he inconspicuously pulled his knife from his belt, Badger turned to face the would-be assailant and began to speak slowly, "I am Badger from Coweta Town. We have returned from the Horseshoe. We are not looking for trouble." Realizing they were very much under the influence of firewater, he was prepared as the first of the men lounged toward him. Reacting quickly, Badger moved his foot, causing the man to fall, cursing as he tumbled to the ground.

What ensued next, instantly brought back images of what happened at the Horseshoe just days before. In only seconds, the dozen vagabond ruffians had rushed the Coweta warriors. Red men and white rolled on the ground, knife blades flashing in the sunlight as it filtered through the moss-covered trees. It seemed as if the white men would overcome the out-numbered warriors, then the unexpected happened.

Making the noise of a thousand devils, the women jumped out of the swamp, each armed with large river cane poles.

They began beating the unsuspecting white men with all their strength. When the surprised men turned to face their attackers, the momentum returned to the warriors who quickly regained control.

Roughly pulling his filthy arms back and forcing the man to his knees, Badger reached to retrieve the knife that had been dropped during the scuffle. One of the men who had not been subdued by the warriors kicked the knife just out of Badger's reach and then jumped on to his back, causing Badger to fall to the ground, losing his hold on the first attacker. Two men now had the warrior penned down. He could smell their vile odor as they evilly grinned at him. Before Badger had time to think what should be done about his predicament, one of the men screamed and slumped over on him. Blood ran down his dirty white arm as the arrow shaft protruded from his shoulder. Startled, the other attacker released Badger. Turning, he was hit squarely in the chest by yet another arrow.

Badger quickly jumped up, his knife in hand. He glanced at the swamp edge, expecting to see reinforcement from other warriors. Instead, he saw the children of Little Flower, each holding their little bows. Wanting to both smile and cry out, he returned to the brawl, realizing that his warriors had all the white volunteer soldiers on the ground with three old worn muskets pointed directly at their heads.

Mocking the leader of the disgusting men, Badger calmly stated, as he surveyed the group, "Look what we have here. A bunch of dirty white soldiers who want to kill an injun or two." Badger looked over at the women as they backed away from the men. "These women of the Red Stick could have killed all of you with only sticks of cane and …." he paused again, laughing, "Little Deer, Red Fox, come out and show yourselves to these brave men." The bushes parted and the two children, still holding their little bows, shyly stepped forward. "As you know, the Red Stick children are very accurate with their aim," Badger continued.

Badger then seriously added, "I do not know who you are or where you plan to go. I strongly suggest that when my warriors release you, there needs to be no hesitation. Just go. Before we were ambushed, I tried to explain to you that we are from Coweta Town and by orders from General Jackson, we were instructed to take these women and children of the Horseshoe to our town. That is what we will do. I warn you. Do not attempt to stop us or harm us in any way. If you do, you will forever remain here in the swamps. That is all I will say," indicating to his warriors to release them, Badger continued, "Now, get out of my sight."

The men slowly rose from the ground, rubbing their arms. With the effects of the firewater having worn off, the boisterous leader picked up his back pack and turned to face Badger. "We mistook you for Red Sticks. We did not plan to kill you, we,"

"Do not lie. Do not force us to kill you. I meant what I said. Go! If darkness finds you here in the swamp, there will be no need for us to kill you," Badger promised.

"We will be on our way. We won't bother you no more. If the big man in Georgie finds out how we attacked you, it will be hell to pay. We just came here to kill them Red Sticks," the leader said as the group of embarrassed men began walking up the path. "I reckon them Red Stick women," he ruefully smiled, "and them children can fight too."

Chapter Nineteen

The White Stick warriors and the Red Stick women waited as the vermin men continued up the path, the low hanging moss quickly hiding them from view. "The only truth to come from his mouth," referring to the final words of the leader of the attackers, Badger turned and smiled. "Thank you. I should have realized the Red Stick women are true fighters. Sunflower Woman, I know you had our backs covered." Badger stooped to take the hands of Little Deer and Red Fox, admitting, "I may owe my life to the two of you. The men standing over me intended to watch me breathe my last."

"Badger, as you have said," Sun Flower Woman began, "We are Red Stick women. We have learned to survive. You are of the White Sticks. Your warriors assisted the white soldiers in destroying our village at the Horseshoe. We have every reason to hate you and to see you die," the strong, brave woman said as moisture formed around her mournful brown eyes. "My people and I also know that you are a good man and that you have much sorrow for what you have done. We trust you now and we know that without your help, we cannot continue to survive or live," pausing to wipe a tear from her eye, she looked at her people as they watched her with pride shinning on their faces. Sunflower Woman spoke again, "We will live and the Spirit of our grandmothers will smile on us."

"Sunflower Woman, I am honored to have your trust and I feel in my heart that the grandmothers will continue to smile on you and your people," Badger said as he looked at the sad, forlorn group who would indeed represent *The Spirit of the Red Stick Women* whose pride, strength and courage would allow them to survive. "I have already sent one of my warriors up the path to make sure the attackers do not back track and return to harm us. I do not think they will, but like most white men, they are not to be trusted."

The sun was directly overhead when the group began their journey toward the Chattahoochee. Without being told, everyone walked at a faster pace toward the east. No time was wasted. Even the children realized the danger of being in the swamp after darkness fell. Badger intended to leave the horse path and move northward and to higher ground. Here they would camp for the night and be ready to start a fresh with the new sun. His group would see Coweta Town before the sun set again.

Chapter Twenty

No further incidents delayed the Red and White Stick travelers as they continued along the path. The sunlight danced through the moss, sparkling on the pools of water that bordered the well-used trail. The cool temperatures prevented the many cottonmouth moccasins which Badger knew lurked underneath the foliage, from showing themselves. The swamp was filled with snakes and alligators as well as the undesirable characters that traversed the trail and was no place for women and children. The most cautious warriors needed to take extreme care to avoid the unseen danger.

Badger was relieved when at last he saw the tiny trail that led out of the swamp. It was good to see the blue sky and feel the cool wind on his face. They had made better time than he had expected and could easily travel farther before making camp for the night. He glanced back over his shoulder and smiled when he saw his charges stop and look at the sky, taking a deep breath of fresh air. "The sun is still high in the sky. We will continue walking if you can," Badger said as the children ran past him.

"We are good and can go as far as necessary," Sunflower Woman said, adding "We are happy to be out of the place that had the smell and feel of evil."

"I was uncomfortable in the swamp too," Badger answered. "We will soon be at a place near a small creek. We will make a fire and prepare food, then sleep. Before the sun sets on the new day, you will see your new home," he promised.

"Yes, we will prepare our minds and hearts for this. We will pray to the Great Spirit to make us strong," Sunflower Woman said as she looked at her people, making sure all of them could continue.

The group resumed their journey, covering the distance Badger had planned in only a short time. The spot near a sparkling little stream was enclosed by long leaf pine and cedar trees, their aroma pleasant and inviting. Some of the children had been asked to gather sticks for the fire while others were told to fill water jars. The Tuckabatchee women had supplied the Red Stick women with basic items, including the jars, an old iron pot, and food they would need to complete their journey to Coweta.

The soothing sounds that indicated the end of day were quickly approaching as the sofkee and bread made from dried corn was eaten. Badger noticed the women, while remaining deeply sorrowful, seemed to be more comfortable and relaxed, and the children playful. He hoped they would be even more at ease when they reached Coweta Town. He knew his people would accept them and treat them kindly.

With the meal finished, preparations were made for the weary travelers to rest and sleep. Golden sage brush cut from the little meadow beyond the pine trees was spread and made excellent beds. Worn blankets had also been supplied by the Tuckabatchee, keeping the Red Stick women and children warm. Badger had posted two of his warriors as guards and he too planned to sleep. Just as he closed his eyes, he heard a rustle in the leaves, his hand instantly reaching for his knife. To his relief, he saw Little Flower quietly sliding through the cedars. Not sure what her intentions were, he allowed her some time for privacy. Standing up, he heard the muffled sound of crying.

"Little Flower," Badger softly called, "Is there something wrong? Why are you crying?"

The moon light was dimly shinning on the beautiful woman's face as she turned to look at Badger. "I am sorry to wake you. I could not sleep. My thoughts are of my husband, Soaring Eagle." Little Flower paused, looking out across the meadow as if she expected to see her husband waiting for her there. "My heart tells me he still lives. I fear if I continue to move away from him, he will not find me." Her small body shook as she gave way to tears.

Badger watched her, wanting again to take her in his arms, but instead, gently took her hand and whispered, "Little Flower, please do not do this to yourself. Soaring Eagle does not live. He gave his life for you, your children, and his people. He fought bravely as the grandfathers would have expected him to do, but he does not live."

With anger flashing in her tear-filled eyes, Little Flower looked up at Badger. "How do you know this? Did you see him die," she demanded?

"No, I did not. Listen to me Little Flower." The White Stick warrior answered, trying to control his emotions. "Only the will of the Giver of Breath could have saved any man at the Horseshoe. I do know that," Badger said as he slowly pulled Little Flower into his arms and held her close as pent-up grief slowly drained from her.

"Little Flower, go back to your children now and sleep. With the new day, you and your people will soon begin a new life in Coweta Town," Badger assured.

****

Chapter Twenty-One

Wolf Fella and the old Red Stick Warriors combed the area in search of anything that could be made into a travois. The severely wounded warrior appeared to be strong enough to be moved. Regardless, he could not be left here. The Red Stick men were not acquainted with the man called Soaring Eagle, but certainly knew of his prowess as the Hillabee Micco.

Two blankets had been quickly bound together with twine and secured to cane poles. The warrior was slowly lifted onto the blankets, crying out in pain with the movement. "Use care," the old warrior called Wolf Fella said, as fresh red stained the already blood soaked shirt.

"Where are we taking him," another one of the warriors asked as he picked up a canteen of water."

"Where ever we go," answered Wolf Fella. "How far to bluff shelter that you talked of earlier," He ask, shifting the travois pole to his other hand.

"Between the Horseshoe and Emuckfa Creek, just off the path on the hillside," the warrior with the musket ball lodged in his arm answered as he gingerly touched his own wound.

Looking up at the bright sun, Wolf Fella nodded his head, "We have time if go now. Take turns carrying travois. Watch for signs of soldiers."

The old warriors were exhausted and the sun was sinking low on the western horizon when they arrived at the bluff shelter. "Here is the shelter," one of the old warriors announced as the travois was easily sat down.

"Go inside to make sure we not be sharing cave with either man nor animal," Wolf Fella instructed the old man at his side. He continued, "As soon as we gather sticks, we make fire. We not have time to look for food. We need to make do with dried corn for now." Wolf Fella squatted down to check on

Soaring Eagle who had remained awake during the journey. His breathing was labored and his face burned hot, but he still lived. "Soaring Eagle, Soaring Eagle," Wolf Fella whispered as he gently touched the man's arm, "We are at safe place now. We do what we can for you."

Soaring Eagle nodded his head slowly, understanding what had been said. "Yes," he answered, barely being heard. "Little Flower, Little Flower, where is," not being able to continue, he closed his eyes and fell into a restless sleep.

"If this man is to live, we must find bear grass to cool heat in his body," Wolf Fella said. "Bear grass grows along streams. I go in search of this." Looking at the other warriors he continued, "Rest of you do what you can to make camp."

Wolf Fella's search was successful, finding the bear grass growing a short distance away. A fire had been started at the entrance of the bluff shelter when he returned and one of the old warriors had startled a rabbit. They would have meat with the dried corn.

They found an old iron pot and filled it with water from the stream. Wolf Fella dropped the entire bear grass plant into the pot, then placed it over the fire. Checking on Soaring Eagle, he respectfully pulled his medicine stick from his belt and began to chant, waving the stick over the body of the injured warrior. He then blew through the hollow stick into the concoction.

The others stood in silence as the old medicine man spoke unfamiliar words from the past. Beads of perspiration formed on his wrinkled face as he retrieved the pot from the fire. He slowly poured the warm liquid into a soldier's canteen and lifted the head of Soaring Eagle. "Drink, you must drink," Wolf Fella demanded as Soaring Eagle tried to swallow the warm potion. After several attempts, the warrior succeeded in drinking enough of the bear grass concoction to satisfy the medicine man. "Now, you sleep," Wolf Fella ordered, sliding the travois closer to the fire. "You get warm, very warm and heat in your body will cool."

Chapter Twenty-Two

The old medicine man sat by the side of the injured warrior long into the night. He watched as Brother Moon rose and climbed high in the sky. He heard the sounds of the hoot owl and the lonesome howl of the coyote. Many times, he bathed the face of Soaring Eagle as he slept, the heat from his body, still hot to his touch. He had quietly repeated the chants and waved his medicine stick, asking the Great Spirit to spare the young warrior. In the dark, silent time of the night before the sky turned gray to welcome the new sun, the old man began to nod and slipped into a deep sleep.

When he awoke, rays of sunshine had begun to filter through the new leaves of the trees. The chirping of the morning birds filled the air and the warrior who had been so close to death, looked intently at the old medicine man.

Surprised, Wolf Fella sat up, embarrassed that he had slept. "Soaring Eagle, you will live. I see life in your eyes." Touching the face of the warrior, Wolf Fella smiled and continued, "Heat gone from body now."

"Water, I need water," Soaring Eagle said in a raspy, weak voice.

Wolf Fella picked up the canteen he had used the night before and quickly ran to the stream for fresh water. "You drink very slowly, too fast make you lose medicine you drank," Wolf Fella said, holding the warrior's head up.

After a few sips of the cold water, Soaring Eagle began to slowly speak. "I saw the trail that leads to the home of the Great Spirit." Closing his eyes, he continued, "I saw my friend Brave Hawk and all of the warriors who died at the Horseshoe." The warrior paused for such a long time, Wolf Fella thought he had slipped back into sleep. When he began to speak again, tears moistened his cheeks. "You are a good medicine maker. You would not allow me to follow the trail to the Great Spirit. For that I thank you," Soaring Eagle finished, looking at Wolf Fella with gratitude.

"You sleep again now. When you wake, I give you stew with rabbit," the old man promised as he smiled at Soaring Eagle.

Chapter Twenty-Three

The midday sunlight danced on the face of Soaring Eagle, waking the sleeping warrior. The musical notes of the mockingbird and the time-of-new-leaves-call of the crow were the only sounds Soaring Eagle heard as he looked around. He saw no one and wondered if he had been left alone. As his eyes adjusted to the bright light, he saw one of the old warriors dozing in the warmth of the sun. In an effort to change position, Soaring Eagle found movement nearly impossible. He gingerly touched his stomach and felt the bear grass leaves that had been placed on top of the ugly gash. He smiled to himself, knowing the old medicine man had again been at work on him.

Hearing the sound of excited voices, Soaring Eagle looked down the hillside and saw the old warrior and two or three younger warriors along with two women, one carrying a small child. As the group came closer to the shelter cave, Soaring Eagle recognized one of the warriors from Hillabee Town, his arm dangling at his side. "Swift Runner, Swift Runner," Soaring Eagle called out in a whisper.

Realizing that he Hillabee Micco had been found, the warrior called Swift Runner hurried to his side and happily exclaimed, "Soaring Eagle, my micco, it is good to see that you live."

"And you Swift Runner," Soaring Eagle managed to say. Looking at the others in the group he continued, "And all of you. Tell me what of the, tell me about...," too weak to finish, Soaring Eagle closed his eyes again.

"Soaring Eagle talk too much," the old medicine man said as he touched the face of the warrior, making sure the heat had not returned to his brow. Satisfied by the cool he felt, he handed two large rabbits to one of the women and directed, "Make stew now and I talk to Soaring Eagle."

Wolf Fella sat down and relayed to Soaring Eagle what had happened. The old warriors had gone in search of food and had also found the group of survivors from the Horseshoe. They too had been hiding in a small shelter cave a short distance away. They had told Wolf Fella of the terrible sights they had seen and the fear they experience as they fled for their lives. The three warriors, too young to be on the battlefield, had been told to protect the women and children. When the soldiers, White Stick Warriors and Cherokees, overtook the village, the youths pulled the two women from the back side of a burning huti. They all suffered minor burns and one of the youths, Swift Runner stumbled, his arm popping as he fell. They had managed to crawl and hid at the edge of a small creek underneath large bushes. They heard the musket fire and the agonizing screams of death. They silently prayed to the Great Spirit that they would not be found. They listened as the sounds of the battle slowly diminished and waited for what seemed an endless time before the soldiers finished their horrible deeds.

Under cover of darkness, the little group, not knowing where to go, had followed the creek and found shelter at a cave. They remained there for several days and had decided to leave as the old warriors found them.

Wolf Fella finished what had been relayed to him by Swift Runner. He watched the emotions that raced across the face of Soaring Eagle, seeing his pain, he began to speak. "When you well enough to move, we go down river. I not know where other Red Sticks are. I not know if any live. All towns could be burned. We go all way to Pensacola Town if need to. We be safe from white soldiers there." The old medicine man warrior moved closer to his patient, checking the knife wound to his stomach, he continued, "You eat rabbit stew and feel better. We talk more then."

The two rabbits mixed with dried corn and wild onions had been enough to satisfy the hunger of the now larger group. After the meal, Wolf Fella moved closer to Soaring Eagle.

Having no tobacco, the old medicine man stuffed his pipe with sumac grass. "Soaring Eagle," he began, "I need you help me get our people to safe place. Make new home. You be well to go two, maybe three suns. We not stay here."

Feeling stronger, the injured warrior slowly pushed himself up until his back rested on the side of a large rock. "Wolf Fella, again, I thank you. The Great Spirit has placed my life in your hands," Soaring Eagle slowly, but clearly said in a much stronger voice. "I know many, if not all of the Red Stick Warriors were killed at the Horseshoe. Can you tell me what happened to the women and children, to my wife, my daughter, my son?" Pausing to catch his breath, he continued, "The soldiers left me for dead. When I was near death, I dreamed that I heard my Little Flower calling for me." The voice of the once-strong warrior broke as tears ran down his face, "My Little Flower, my Flower."

Wolf Fella placed his hand on the warrior to calm him. "Soaring Eagle not need talk so much, not move. Women and children and old men," patting his chest to indicate himself, "all made hostage. Old men escape. White Stick Warriors take others to Tuckabatchee Town and Coweta Town on Chattahoochee." The old medicine man smiled, continuing, "Wife and children go. Warrior called Badger take good care."

The look of joyful anticipation that had appeared on the face of Soaring Eagle quickly turned to one of anger. Frowning, Soaring Eagle stated emphatically, "In two suns, we will go to Tuckabatchee town to find my Flower and my children."

Spirit of the Red Stick Women

Chapter Twenty-Four

With the continued applications from the old medicine man, Soaring Eagle healed quickly. In two suns, he, the old warriors, and the little group of refugees were ready to go in search of other Red Stick survivors. Each town they came to had been partially burned and ransacked. There was no sign of any of the people who had made the villages their home, except for those who no longer lived. The old warriors had hurriedly buried the bodies of the slain and moved on to the next town to repeat the process again.

The sun had slid well below the horizon and shadows had begun to fall before the fatigued travelers stopped to make camp. Enduring much pain, Soaring Eagle managed to keep up with the others. He wanted desperately to be reunited with his family.

Enough food had been salvaged from the towns they had passed through to provide a sufficient meal and a few more blankets had been picked up. No one would be cold or hungry. As the others prepared to sleep, Soaring Eagle and Wolf Fella sat in silence. The smoke from their pipes encircling both the old warrior and the younger micco. Wolf Fella, looking deeply into the fire, began to speak words of the ancient ones. He spoke slowly, the unfamiliar words lulling Soaring Eagle into a trance-like state, taking him to a different place and time, where he too understood the words of the grandfathers.

Wolf Fella, just as slowly, began speaking in his familiar way and Soaring Eagle snapped back into the present. Rubbing his eyes, the confused warrior asked, "What just happened to me? I feel as if I have been with the grandfathers."

"You have been with the grandfathers. Words of ancient ones help you understand future," the old medicine man answered as he reached out to touch the arm of Soaring Eagle.

He continued, "You now know you will have long life. You will face much pain and see much sadness. You will lead our people well. That what grandfathers say. Now, we sleep. Go far in new day."

Chapter Twenty-Five

The group did manage to go far the following day. They crossed the muddy waters of Turtle Rattle Creek and planned to go even farther before making camp for the night. Wolf Fella stopped and made the sign of silence. Soaring Eagle saw them first and reached for his knife while holding his hand out to stop the others. A ragged group of four Red Stick Warriors cautiously stepped from the cover of bushes that lined the creek. They all suffered from various minor wounds and injuries and seemed extremely tired. The taller of the group, a gash on his arm still red and ugly, looked at Soaring Eagle, recognizing him as the Hillabee Micco.

"Micco, I am called War Singer. My town is Fish Pond. We," pointing at the other warriors, "We go to Horseshoe," he paused, "We too late. Sharp Knife Jackson is on the path near river on way to fort where Oakfuskee meets the Coosa," the warrior said breathlessly.

"How do you know this," Soaring Eagle asked, placing his knife back in his belt.

"We get close to soldier camp and hear talk. Other white soldiers come this path. We need to move quickly. They not far behind," War Singer said.

Frowning, Soaring Eagle looked at his group, seeing their fatigue. "We will go. There is a smaller path up the creek that we can take. We will use care to leave no trail where we walk. It will be longer to Tuckabatchee Town. I do not think the soldiers will go this way."

"We not go to Tuckabatchee Town. Bad soldiers say they go there before go home. Want to drink firewater," War Singer said.

"We will go to Tuckabatchee Town," Soaring Eagle replied, almost angrily. "My family is there."

Seeing the anger in the micco's face, War Singer answered quietly. "Soaring Eagle, we are Red Stick Warriors. Tuckabatchee is a white peace town. We will be killed if we go there. You know I speak truth."

Rubbing his weary eyes, Soaring Eagle nodded his head in agreement. "You are speaking the truth War Singer. I spoke from my heart, not my head." Looking perplexed, he continued, "Where will we go?"

"Hear soldiers say Red Sticks go to Pensacola Town in place called Florida. They not follow there," War Singer said, touching the cut on his arm.˙.When did you get injured if you did not fight at the Horseshoe," Soaring Eagle asked.

"We had little battle with few white men who want to kill injuns they say. We smell them first," War Singer continued, "They kill no more injuns."

Soaring Eagle nodded his head in understanding and declared, "I will find my family. First, we will go to Pensacola Town."

Chapter Twenty-Six

Soaring Eagle and the old warriors along with the young warriors and women, had made the long, hard journey to the town of Pensacola. The trip had taken much longer than anticipated, the group encountering much difficulty along the way. They continued to see the abandoned, partially burned villages and the desolate fields where corn had not been planted in two seasons of new leaves. They had detoured around Tuckabatchee and other white towns of peace, hoping to avoid contact with any who would do them harm. Capture had been barely avoided when they ventured too near a white farmstead on the Conecuh River, the group, having to flee under cover of darkness, to avoid contact.

Soaring Eagle was recovering from his injuries and had assumed the position as leader of the group which now numbered more than twenty. Several Red Stick Warriors who had not been at the Horseshoe but hid in the cane breaks after their towns had been attacked, gladly joined with the little group. Many of their families had already been taken to Pensacola.

The tired and hungry group of Red Sticks stood in amazement as the bustling town came into view. None of them had ever seen such a sight before. Traders hawking their wares from big houses made of rock, horses pulling wagons over paths made of stone and people all around. White, black, and red mingled together, each one talking in a different language. Looking at the scene before him, one of the warriors shook his head and asked the question all of them were thinking, "What place is this? What we do? Maybe go back in woods."

Soaring Eagle knew he had to take control and calm his people. Forcing a smile, he began talking, "We are in the town of the white people who are friendly to us. Do not fear, we will look for others who are also Red Sticks." Looking around for someone to ask where they should go, he continued, "Stay close and be silent. Follow me."

Soaring Eagle and his little group of warriors continued walking, becoming more comfortable as they went along the street. They realized that no one intended them any harm. Hearing his name called from across the crowd, Soaring Eagle turned to see Peter McQueen walking toward him.

"Soaring Eagle, my friend," the Red Stick leader said, clasping the warrior's arm. "It is good to see you live. I did not know if you survived the Horseshoe. I was told so many of our warriors did not."

"Peter, it is good to see you as well. The Great Spirit has smiled on me," Soaring Eagle answered, equally glad to see his friend.

McQueen looked at the others, seeing the women and children, "Come, I will take you to join our people. I know you need food and rest. Then we will talk more," the Red Stick leader said, as he led the way, weaving between white and red people on the crowded cobblestone street.

Chapter Twenty-Seven

"Why is the river called Flowered Rocks?" Little Deer asked. "Do flowers grow in the water?" Laughing at the little girl who continued to amuse and surprise him with her intelligence and bravery, Badger answered, "Yes, flowers do grow on the rocks and the rocks also have the shape of a flower. Come, I will show you." Badger took the child's hand and led her to the bank of the Chattahoochee River. Standing on a large boulder that extended from the water, he picked Little Deer up and pointed into the slow-moving water. "See, the rocks and the flowers?"

"Yes, I do see," the child said sadly as tears formed in her eyes.

"Little Deer, why are you crying," Badger asked as he helped her down from the boulder. "Do you not think the river of Flowered Rocks is pretty?"

"Yes, it is pretty, she whispered in a soft little voice, "Can my father find us here? I know he will look."

Badger looked at the broken-hearted child wanting to make her smile again, but realizing she needed to know the truth. "Little Deer, do you remember when we left the Horseshoe and I told you and your brother that," pausing, taking her hands in his, "that your father was a brave warrior and he has made the grandfathers proud, but I do not think that he still lives," The troubled warrior said as he brushed the tears from her face.

With a defiant look, Little Deer said with a voice of maturity that startled Badger, "Yes, I remember and you also said that you will help us look for him. Do you remember?" The child demanded, "My father still lives and I know that! Please take me back to my family and tell us what you wish for us to do."

Badger and Little Deer walked the short distance to the village. He had been excited to answer the child's questions about the name of the great river that flowed through his town by showing her the rocks that lay just beneath the surface. Realizing he should have first taken the time to settle the Horseshoe refugees into their new home, he was glad to see they had gotten a much better welcome here than at Tuckabatchee. The women and children had already been brought food and his people were treating them with much kindness. Nodding his head in approval, the warrior said, "This is good." He then went in search of the Coweta Micco.

Chapter Twenty-Eight

Before the sun set behind the large stand of virgin pine trees that bordered the white peace town of Coweta, the refugees from the Tallapoosa had been placed in their new homes. Everyone would be treated well, mothers and their children were not separated. They would be expected to help with the many chores of daily life and contribute to the well-being of the town.

Little Flower and the twins were chosen by the kind, gentle mother of Badger and Sun Flower woman would live in the nearby huti of her sister. The two women had much in common and quickly bonded, becoming friends. Working together, the evening meal was prepared and the Horseshoe refugees seemed to relax and for the first time in many days, were not afraid.

"My mother, these people who live on the Flowered Rocks River are kind," Little Deer said as she finished her meal of fish and sofkee. "They are much like us, except some of them dress as the whites do."

"Yes, we will be treated well here," Little Flower answered her daughter, smiling as her son rushed by, a new friend at his side.

"We will, but this is not our home. When will we return to the Fawn River and search for my father. I think it will be hard for him to find us here," the beautiful little girl said, looking up at her mother, her brown eyes shining with unshed tears.

"My Child," Little Flower said, surprised at the words of her daughter. "You have much wisdom for one who has seen so few seasons. We will return to the Tallapoosa when the time is right and we will be reunited with your father. I know in my heart too that he still lives. We will need to be patient. There is much danger still. I promise you my brave little one that we will someday return to our home."

Badger had returned from his talk with the Coweta Micco and the headmen and had heard the conversation between Little Flower and her daughter. The words saddened him, but he understood that only time would heal the wounds of this family who had lost so much. He also hoped he would be allowed to help them find happiness again.

He turned to the older woman who was still busy trying to make her new family comfortable. "My mother, it is good that you and all of my people are showing such kindness to our friends from the Horseshoe." Badger looked in the iron pot dangling over the fire. "Did you save some food for your son," he exclaimed, laughing, pulling his mother to him in a bear hug. "I have missed your cooking."

Sings Softly Woman returned her son's hug. "I have missed you my son. My heart is glad that you have returned safely," She said as she filled a large bowl with sofkee and removed a slab of fish and bread from the large rocks that encircled the fire. "Your friends are now my family and they will be welcome to stay here for as long as they wish."

"Do you live here too," the now familiar voice of Little Deer suddenly asked as Badger ate his sofkee.

"No, I live in the lodge of the warriors. I do come here to eat when I am hungry. My mother makes good sofkee," Badger said, smiling at his mother over the little girl's head.;

"You do not have a wife and sons and daughters," Little Deer questioned in the inquisitive way of a small child.

Badger shook his head and quickly looked away from Little Deer and her mother who saw the sadness that covered his face.

"Little Deer, do not ask so many questions. That does not concern you," Little Flower admonished, embarrassed that her child was so forward with the warrior.

"Do not scold the child," Badger said, a warm smile returning to his handsome face. "She is curious and how else can she learn if she does not ask."

"My children have been taught the ways of the grandmothers," Little Flower said. "She has been taught to show respect and to be," trying not to smile herself, she continued, "to be silent unless spoken to."

"Little Deer, silent," Badger queried. With that both Badger as well as Little Flower broke out in laughter. "This child has too much energy and excitement. She will never be silent," Badger paused for a moment, his face sobering, "She and I are great friends. Remember, I have saved her life and she has saved mine. We share a bond, one that will last for as long as the sun shines." He passed the bowl back to his mother for a refill, knowing that she had listened to the conversation with interest. Badger continued, "Please sit down. I would like to tell the family of Sun Flower Woman about the White Stick Warrior who is known as Badger, and of the woman I call my mother."

Red Fox, hearing the laughter, had returned to the circle of women as Badger softly began to talk.

"It was in the time of the cold moon, I had not seen as many seasons as the two of you," he looked at the wide-eyed children and continued, "My father and mother along with me and my younger sister, lived much farther up the Chattahoochee. Our village was small and at times we were hungry. Our micco, who was the brother of my father, said that we should move down river to a larger village. On the second day of our journey, we were attacked by Uchee warriors." Badger paused, a brief shadow covered his face as he was filled with memories from the long ago past. "My father was killed and my mother and sister were taken hostage. I have not seen them since. I was left for dead. I was found by the husband of my mother." He pointed to the older woman who looked at him with adoring eyes. "They treated me as their own son, teaching me the ways of the Coweta." Badger looked at the woman he now called mother. "Should I continue my Mother, or have I told my new friends all they need to know?"

"My son, I will complete your story, for they should know of the goodness of your heart," Sings Softly Woman said as she refilled Red Fox's bowl with hot sofkee. "The grieving child soon became the favorite of Coweta Town. He has always put the good of the people before his own needs, many times supplying food for the old and the sick." She smiled, continuing, "I remember when he received his warrior name. He had gone with his father, my husband, to the far north country to make trades. They were gone many suns. I was much afraid. When they returned, I was told this story. It was in the cold season. They happened on a family of badgers. Fearing for her babies, the mother quickly latched herself onto the toe of the moccasin of my son." Beginning to laugh, she continued, "He was in much pain, but he calmly stuck a stick in the mouth of the badger, releasing the grip. The mother badger then gathered up her family and scampered away. That is how my son became known as Badger."

"Can I see your toe," Red Fox asked. "Did the animal bite it off?"

"No, I still have my toe, but I was afraid to look. I do still have a scare where her teeth sunk into my big toe," Badger said as he removed his moccasin, "See!"

Becoming solemn again, Sings Softly Woman resumed the story of her son. "My son continued with his good ways, gaining the confidence of the micco and the elders. It was then time for him to take a wife."

The expression of pain again appeared on the face of the warrior. "Mother, let us not talk of this now. I am sure there has been enough said of me. I would rather hear about my little friends," Badger said, rubbing the head of Red Fox.

"I want to know of your family," Little Deer said, sliding closer to Badger.

"Little Deer, do you not remember what I told you," Little Flower said, scolding her daughter, again. "This is of no concern to us. Now, you apologize and then you and your brother should gather sticks for the night fire."

"Yes, mother, I am sorry to ask so many questions," the child replied, smiling sweetly at Badger, "I would like to know."

Unable to resist the child, Badger returned her smile. "Little Deer, you are relentless! I will briefly tell you about the family I had for much too short of time." Badger sat back down and looked at his mother, who tenderly and quietly encouraged her son.

"Her name was Yellow Bird," Badger began. "She was the most beautiful of all the maidens in Coweta Town. She had eyes for only me and I looked at no other. She became my wife during the time of new corn. We would have only two seasons together," Badger paused, remembering the young woman who had given him such happiness.

The body of Yellow Bird was small, too small to give birth to our child. My son was born on a night when brother moon was big. There was no one to provide his nourishment," taking a deep breath, he continued, "The child did not live for the next big moon to shine on him. That is all," the emotional warrior said as he stood and walked away from the saddened family.

"Six seasons have passed and my son still has not taken another wife. I pray to the Giver of Breath that will soon change," Sings Softly Woman said, looking at the little family before her. "He will make a good husband and father."

Chapter Twenty-Nine

In only a few suns the refugees from the Horseshoe had settled into their new home. While still in their time of mourning, they were more at peace and had accepted the will of the Great Spirit. The twins had easily made friends with the Coweta children and spent their free time at play. The friendship of Sun Flower Woman and the sister of the mother of Badger continued to grow. Little Flower stayed busy during the day, trying not to think of the sorrow and great loss she, the Hillabee and many other Creek people had experienced. Her nights were difficult, longing for the arms of Soaring Eagle. The heart broken woman cried herself to sleep only waking to again realize that he was not there.

Badger watched the beautiful woman, understanding her pain. He knew that only time would heal her broken heart. He was also concerned about her well-being. She had no appetite, eating very little and the dark circles under her eyes seemed to grow larger every day. He knew her daily routine included going to the little creek that merged into the wide river. After filling her water bottles, she would sit and watch as the two waters became one.

He had followed her again, deciding this would be the day he would tell of his feelings for her. He realized she would reject his words, telling him that her husband still lived. If she would only listen to him and accept the truth, he knew that he could make her smile again. They would not be allowed to become man and wife for many moons, not until Busk, that would give her more time. If only he could just talk to her.

Taking a deep breath, Badger separated the tall river cane that lined the creek. Hearing the movement, Little Flower quickly turned to see the nervous warrior.

"Badger, you startled me," Little Flower said as she quickly wiped the tears from her dark eyes. "Does your mother need me to help her?"

Spirit of the Red Stick Women

"No, Little Flower, it is not my mother that needs you," stopping before he continued, Badger silently thought to himself, "It is me that needs you." "I have words to say to you," Badger quietly said.

"Badger," the beautiful woman began.

"Little Flower, please listen to what I have to say." Feeling more confident, Badger continued, "You know now of the family I briefly had. I have not looked upon another woman since. I could not. Little Flower, try to understand what I say now. I have feelings for you," he paused as tears began to sparkle in her eyes, "and I care for your children. I did not know I could feel this way again. Please let me help you to find happiness."

"Badger," Little Flower replied as she took his hand. "Badger, I know of your feelings for me and I know you are fond of my children. I also know you understand why I cannot accept happiness from you. I love my husband and I know that he lives and we will be together again. You said yourself that you could not look upon another woman until," looking away from the warrior who was watching her intently, Little Flower smiled and bravely said, "I cannot look upon another man. I value your friendship and I appreciate the kindness you show my children. I cannot promise you anything more."

Fully expecting that response from her, Badger surprised her and himself when he leaned over and kissed her cheek, brushing the glistening tears from her sad, forlorn but beautiful face.

"Little Flower, I do understand. I want you to understand too that I love you and if the plans you have for your future do not happen, then I will be there for you." Feeling relived that she had not shown anger at his words or actions, he pulled her to her feet. "I have just one more request and I promise I will not speak of this again," he smiled, "unless it is your wish." Becoming serious again, he continued, "Please, do not have eyes for another. Now, return to our town. My mother will have chores for you."

****

Chapter Thirty

Soaring Eagle and his little group of refugees from the Horseshoe followed Peter McQueen to the outskirts of the sprawling white-man town of Pensacola. Never had they experienced so much clamor or witnessed such a spectacle. People of various colors roamed the streets by the dozens. Words of English, French, Choctaw, Muscogee, and the African man echoed across the cobble-stoned streets, each man trying to out talk the other, the noise was deafening.

"Peter, where did these men come from," Soaring Eagle asked his leader. "Why are they all speaking at one time?"

Laughing, the Red Stick warrior answered, "We will soon leave this town of confusion and return to the quiet of the forests."

"Why is the smell of salt so strong," one of the young warriors from Hillabee Town asked. "And the constant sound of water lapping, where is that coming from?"

Peter laughed again as he parted a large clump of green bushes that grew as tall as the warriors. "Look."

The group stopped just short of the Red Stick warrior, gasping as the sight of the great water came into view. "This is the ocean, the big water the white man talks about. The water that brings their boats to our land," McQueen explained.

Frightened, the women and children began hiding behind the warriors. "I fear this ocean. It is coming closer. Can we leave this place," one of them said?

"Yes, it is fearful to see the big water for the first time. Our camp is in the other direction, but the sound of the big water can still be heard," Peter McQueen said. "It will not be so fearful there. Come, there is food for all of us."

Chapter Thirty-One

The Red Stick leader, Peter McQueen led the fatigued and hungry travelers away from the big water, deeper into the grove of palm trees and scrub bushes. They were amazed, not only at the enormous town with the many different faces and colors of people, but also the strange terrain of the land.

"What tree is this," the same inquisitive young warrior asked. "And there is white sand everywhere. It is in my nose and in my eyes."

McQueen smiled again at the young warrior's inexperience and answered, "They are called palm trees and they grow only near the big water. The sand comes from the water too, as it rushes in and out to meet the land."

After walking for only a short time, an opening came into view. Muscogee warriors from many towns, some still wearing the identifying red feathers in their hair, sat in little groups, smoking their pipes, and talking with much animation. Their women and children were busy at various tasks of meal preparation.

"Soaring Eagle, come with me," the Red Stick warrior said, gesturing for the others to sit down. "Sofkee and bread will be prepared soon."

The two warriors walked toward a group of men sitting near the edge of the large encampment. Their loud voices indicating that they were in a heated discussion.

"Josiah, Patty, Jim," McQueen called out, interrupting the conversation. "This is Soaring Eagle, Micco of the Hillabee. He was at the Horseshoe. Soaring Eagle, I am sure you know of Josiah Francis, Patty Welse and Jim Boy."

The three warriors stood, each clasping the forearm of the young micco.

"I have heard much of your prowess," Soaring Eagle said, returning the traditional greeting of warriors, pausing as he gripped the strong arm of the latter. "Jim Boy, I heard the news from down river that you had walked the path to the Great Spirit at Calebee during the time of the cold moon."

"Many of our brave warriors did walk the path," Jim Boy confirmed. "It was not my time. I was confused with another from Cusseta Town who had the same name as me. As you see, I lived and I will fight again."

"Sit and tell us of the Horseshoe. Tell us of the battle and how many of our brave men were lost," Francis said as he sat back down.

"We will wait to hear of the battle after our friend has food. He has walked far and will need to rest as well," McQueen said, frowning at the impatience of the warrior.

"Peter, as soon as I eat some sofkee, I will be ready to tell of the horrible battle and the great loss of our people," Soaring Eagle promised, gratefully accepting a steaming bowl of sofkee from one of the women who had overheard his request.

Quickly finishing his food, Soaring Eagle began to talk. "The barricade was strong," looking at the seasoned warriors sitting across from him. "You saw it before you left. We did not think Sharp Knife Jackson could break through the thick logs. We did not know the Creek and Cherokee, who were not our friends, would cross the Oakfuskee and take the canoes that were intended for our escape and instead fill them with white soldiers, the soldiers who attacked the village and," his voice breaking, "took our women and children." Willing himself not to think of his family, the sorrow filled warrior continued, "We knew we would be out-numbered and Jackson would have his big guns. We exchanged fire, our arrows and his bullets soaring harmlessly overhead, striking no one. Some of the soldiers bravely came closer to the barricade," Soaring Eagle smiled wryly, "and quickly turned back as some of our arrows came too close to the target! This continued until we noticed smoke coming from the village. Sharp Knife also saw the smoke and at that point his soldiers rushed the barricade. What ensued next, I cannot bring myself to talk of now, possibly never. Our warriors, my friends fought bravely, honoring the grandfathers well. Then they began to drop all around me and I felt the sharp edge of a knife enter my stomach. As I was falling to the ground, I looked up to see the ugly, evil face of a white soldier as he struck my head with the butt of his musket. I was left for dead and would be, if not for the will of the Great Spirit and that old medicine man over there." Soaring Eagle stopped, pointing to the man who had indeed saved his life.

"Soaring Eagle," Josiah Francis asked, "Do you have any idea how many of our warriors were lost? Where did the soldiers take the women and children?"

Before Soaring Eagle could answer, Jim Boy quickly asked, "Have you heard where Jackson and his soldiers were going after the Horseshoe?"

"Jackson has divided his soldiers. They have gone in each direction, burning villages as they go," pausing, Soaring Eagle looked at each of the Red Stick Warriors," our numbers have been greatly diminished. Most of the strongest and the bravest have taken the path to the Great Spirit. It has been told to me, that the women and children were taken north by the Cherokee, some to the place called Big Spring. Others were taken by White Sticks down the Tallapoosa to Tuckabatchee and then over to the Chattahoochee," pausing, he continued in almost a whisper, "My wife and children have been taken there by a White Stick Warrior that goes by the name of Badger. I will go there and find this man and my family."

McQueen and the other warriors had listened in silence to the words of Soaring Eagle. Frowning, he touched the shoulder of the tired man, seeing the sorrow in his eyes. "My friend, we will go with you to find your family. First, we must gather up the remaining Red Stick Warriors. We have heard from others who came to this place that many are still hidden in the woods and cane breaks. There are still battles to be fought. We are not finished with the white skin people who wish to seize our women and take our land."

"No, I have experienced the horrors of battle. I have killed the white man and I have seen those around me die the valiant death of the mighty warrior. I have seen the path that leads to the Great Spirit. It was not yet my time to go. I will fight the battles with the white man no more. I will go to my family and we will live in peace," Soaring Eagle proclaimed defiantly.

Francis, Welse and Jim Boy all rose to their feet in anger. Welse was the first to speak. "Soaring Eagle, you are one of us. You cannot decide you do not want to fight!"

"Are you a coward," Francis yelled, his eyes flashing. "Do you wish to hide behind the skirts of your woman?"

McQueen, seeing the anger in the eyes of his friends and realizing what they were capable of doing in the heat of the moment, quickly stepped in between them and Soaring Eagle. "Francis, Jim, Patty, calm down. We will talk this over. There is no reason for anger here. Soaring Eagle is one of us. He has suffered and lost much. He needs to rest and clear his mind. We will talk of this when the sun is new." Turning to Soaring Eagle, he continued, "Go now and rest with your people."

Soaring Eagle nodded at the warriors glaring at him, noticing that Francis had placed his hand on his knife. "Thank you, Peter, I am very tired. We will talk with the new day."

Chapter Thirty-Two

Many more Creek refugees, mostly women and children from villages on the Tallapoosa and Coosa Rivers had straggled into the Red Stick camp overnight. All of them were ragged and hungry. As the self-imposed leader of the rapidly growing camp, the new comers looked to Peter McQueen for shelter and to provide them with food. He looked around the camp, shocked at the number of people for which he was now somewhat responsible. The Spanish Governor had already told him that food supplies were running low and he and his people could not stay in Pensacola indefinitely. His plans were to fight the white man and to save the land of his people, not to provide food for them. This should be the responsibility of someone else.

The sun had risen well into the morning sky before he had the opportunity to again speak with Soaring Eagle. McQueen had spent much of the night thinking of ways to solve the predicament that the Hillabee Micco had presented. He understood why Soaring Eagle no longer had the stomach to fight. Francis and Jim considered him weak and a coward and understood nothing.

As McQueen stood and viewed the vast group of people, a thought occurred to him. If Soaring Eagle were willing, it would solve this dilemma. Smiling as he approached him, McQueen greeted the micco, "Ah, Soaring Eagle, you look rested. I trust you had a good night."

"Yes, Peter, I slept well. I see more of our people have joined your camp," Soaring Eagle said as he too looked over the large number of refugees who all seemed to be occupied with some sort of chore. "Peter, what will you do with so many? How will you feed them? I am not surprised that so few of them are warriors."

"Yes, more came in during the darkness and they all were hungry," McQueen laughed. "Come Soaring Eagle, walk with me."

The two warriors walked to the outskirts of the encampment. Neither spoke until the ocean came into view, the water shinning brilliantly as it rushed into the while shore.

"This is an amazing sight. I feel so small," Soaring Eagle said as he took a deep breath of salt-filled air.

Peter McQueen answered sadly, "Yes, it is much different from our home on the Tallapoosa. I would rather be there than here. That is not possible now. He continued, "Soaring Eagle, about our conversation last night."

"Peter," Soaring Eagle interrupted, "I have a clear mind now. I still will not fight the war with the white man. If you would like for me and my people to leave, then we will do so."

"Soaring Eagle, I too have thought much about what you have said. I do understand, but my friends Francis, Jim and even Patty do not. They intend to fight to the end, as I do." McQueen said as he stooped to pick up a large conch shell. "I have a plan which I think will work for both of us."

"Tell me of your plan, Peter, "Soaring Eagle said, taking the shell from him. "My son and daughter would like to have one of these. Can we find more?"

"Yes, there are many scattered along the shore. We can look as we talk. Soaring Eagle, I have a problem that you may be able to help with. You spoke of all our people who have converged here. I cannot harbor so many people. I have no way to supply food and the Spanish Governor has told me his food supply is short," McQueen explained.

"What can I do to help with this problem," Soaring Eagle asked, frowning.

"When you leave, and I think for your own safety that you should, it would be of great help if you would take as many as you can with you," McQueen said as he watched a flock of seagulls swoop down in from of them.

"Peter, where will we go and how will I feed more people?

There is no food to be found," Soaring Eagle lamented.

"Your family is on the Chattahoochee. Is that correct?" McQueen asked, feeling hope that the micco was willing to listen to him.

"Yes, at the Town of Coweta," Soaring Eagle answered, puzzled.

"If you travel within the interior, staying inside the Spanish territory until you reach the water of the Flowered Rocks, you will be safe from the white soldiers. Once on the river, you can travel north to Coweta," McQueen informed his friend.

"What about the others I will have with me? You still have not told me about food for them," Soaring Eagle inquired.

"There are many towns of the Seminole scattered along the way. They will take many of the women and children. The few warriors who want to fight can remain with me," McQueen finished, "If your path crosses that of other Red Stick Warriors, tell them to come here. As I told you, there are still battles to fight."

"I have twenty people with me, three or four of the young warriors may desire to stay with you," Soaring Eagle said as he wiped the wisp of sand from his face. "How many more would need to go?"

"If you can take twenty or twenty-five of the women and children, that would help me immensely," McQueen said as he stopped to pick up yet another large shell. "I can give you enough food to last a day or maybe two. By then, you will have reached a Seminole town. As I said, a few of the women and their children can be left at each town."

"When do I leave? And, I will also need some directions of travel, remember that I have never been so near the big water," Soaring Eagle said as he looked out over the ocean. "I too had much rather be on the Tallapoosa and I intend to go back."

"My friend, I hope that you can find your family and that you will be able to go back to your home. I fear things will not be the same," McQueen stated, clasping the forearm of Soaring Eagle, while actually admiring the man. "It will take courage to do this just as it takes courage to fight. I think you should leave as soon as we prepare the people to go. As for as directions to the Chattahoochee, I will send one of my young men to guide you and he can bring back any warriors who wish to fight. I will not talk with you again, as I must meet with the governor. He has promised more guns and ammunition. I think the man speaks with a forked tongue. He will regret it if he does not speak the truth to me," The Red Stick leader said as he turned back to the camp. "Oh yes, give these shells to your children, the prettiest one to the little girl. I remember she showed no fear when I passed through your town before the battles began."

"Yes, my daughter has the *Spirit of the Red Stick Women* just like her mother and grandmother. Thank you, Peter McQueen. I will find my family and we will go home. May the Great Spirit be with you," Soaring Eagle said to the man he considered his friend. This would be the final time the two of them would have words. Fate would not allow them to meet again.

Chapter Thirty-Three

The sun was directly overhead when Soaring Eagle and his group of refugees along with twenty-five additional women and children left the noisy frontier town of Pensacola. No one resisted the move to yet another unknown destination. They would go where they were told as long as food was provided. They did not realize that the rationed corn and fish wrapped in palm leaves that each had been given, was all the food they would have for several days.

The guide McQueen had sent with them seemed very young and inexperienced to Soaring Eagle. He doubted if the young dark-skinned warrior could lead them very far before all of them became hopelessly lost. Bear Killer did seem confident in his ability to guide as he headed up the path away from the encampment of the Red Stick Warriors. Turning once to beckon them on, the young warrior acted as if he were starting off on a great adventure.

Soaring Eagle had given orders that everyone should keep up and that there would be no stopping until camp was made for the night. He brought up the rear of the group, encouraging the stragglers to make haste. Soaring Eagle noticed that a grandmother with two small children seemed to be having problems getting the little ones to walk. "Grandmother, can these children not walk any faster? We are falling behind the others," he spoke in a kindly way.

The old woman looked at the warrior, tears streaming down her worn, wrinkled face. "They have no moccasins. Their feet are cut and bruised and I am unable to carry both," the old woman cried as she showed Soaring Eagle her burned arm still covered with blisters.

Startled to see the injury, Soaring Eagle asked, "Grandmother, how did you receive this burn and what is your town?"

"My town is," wiping the tears from her eyes, she continued, "was Oakfuskee. We were told we would be safe there. After the Horseshoe, the soldiers came and most of the town was torched. My name is Dancing Woman. These are the children of my daughter. She gave her life so that her children could live. I received my injury when I pulled them from their burning huti. We hid in the woods for many suns. We were found by our warriors and brought here. That was during the darkness of the night. I am so tired, I do not know if I can go any farther. Please take the children and make sure they are safe. They have no one. Their father and uncle were at the Horseshoe." The tired old woman slumped over against a palm tree. She began to cough and bright red blood trickled from her mouth. Soaring Eagle watched in horror as the old woman slowly took her last breath.

The medicine man was among the last to leave the encampment and had observed what had happened. He rushed over to the old woman, declaring that she no longer lived. The two children, boys having seen only five or six seasons, both began to cry for their grandmother. Soaring Eagle tried without success to comfort them. After calling for some of the women to come back for the boys, he and the medicine man carried the body of the woman to the side of the path and quickly buried her. As Soaring Eagle placed two large palm branches over the grave, the medicine man spoke words of the ancient ones, sending the grandmother down the path of the Great Spirit. Turning to look at the warrior, he added, "Soaring Eagle, along path of our people, there will be many graves. You need to be strong to guide them. Let us go now, we have far to travel."

****

Chapter Thirty-Four

The season of new leaves had slowly turned into the time of harvest. The people of Coweta along with their new families from the Horseshoe had worked together planting corn and beans. While many in the Creek Nation would be hungry, there would be ample food for their town. The Red Stick people had no towns in which to plant their corn and needed to move from place to place in order to survive. Small groups of refugees from the Tallapoosa River Valley continued to be brought to Coweta Town. All of them were welcome and placed in homes of the women.

Preparations for the Green Corn Ceremony were underway and everyone, including the children, were expected to contribute in some way. Little Deer and Red Fox had been told to help gather corn from one of the large fields on the outskirts of the town. As the two filled the cane baskets with the golden silked corn, the clamor of voices was heard coming from the path from Tuckabatchee.

The children watched with curiosity as a small group of women and children were led past the field of corn into the town. "Look, Red Fox, is that woman the wife of our uncle? Is that Spotted Fawn and her family," Little Deer excitedly asked.

"Yes, it is, hurry, let us go tell our mother," Red Fox answered as he picked up his side of the basket.

"Mother, mother," the excited twins screamed in unison as they ran to Little Flower who was busy combining a lump of orange-colored clay with sand.

Being accustomed to the excitement of her children, Little Flower turned to them and smiled, "My children, why are you so excited this day? Have you completed your job of gathering corn?"

"Yes, mother, see our basket is full," Little Deer replied.

Seeing the ears of fresh corn that had fallen from the basket as the children ran, Little Flower laughed, "I think you should go back and pick up what was dropped. Now, what did you want to tell me?"

"We saw Spotted Fawn and her children," Red Fox said.

"Spotted Fawn, where," Little Flower asked. "Are you sure?"

"She and some other women were just brought into the village," Little Deer answered, pointing, "See, over there.

Little Flower watched as several women and children, their clothing tattered and dirty, followed a couple of old warriors. Dropping the clay mixture, the now excited woman ran to greet the woman she loved as a sister and had not seen since the Horseshoe, shouting, "Spotted Fawn, Spotted Fawn!"

"Little Deer, oh, Little Deer," Spotted Fawn cried, falling into the arms of her friend, tears streaming down her face.

"Spotted Fawn," Little Deer exclaimed, wiping her own tears, "I did not think you still lived."

And I was sure that you did not," Spotted Fawn admitted.

The two women stood clinging to each other as the village people gathered around the group.

"I think these women and children need to eat," the strong voice of the mother of Badger was then heard over the crying and now laughter of the younger women. "Come, Little Flower, tell us who your friends are."

The motley group of women and children, along with the two old warriors, had wandered from place to place, finding only fear and hunger in every village. They continued to move, hoping to find clan or family members who could help them. They had been told that some of the people from the Horseshoe had been taken to the Chattahoochee and if they could make it that far, they would be given shelter. The tired group rejoiced when the Coweta Warriors discovered them wandering in the woods, a short distance from the village.

Chapter Thirty-Five

The most recent group of refugees from the Horseshoe were soon absorbed into the Coweta Town, finding homes with clan members. Spotted Fawn and her children were assigned to a family of the Deer Clan who lived on the opposite side of the village from Little Flower. The two women could not spend as much time together as they would have liked, but the bond between them quickly became strong again.

Preparations for the Green Corn Ceremony had neared completion and would begin with the new sun. The ceremony, which was a time of renewal, and the reuniting with Spotted Fawn, had created a feeling of melancholy for Little Flower. Using the excuse to fill the water bottles, Little Flower walked down the path to the large spring. She had hoped to have time alone to reflect on the events that had happened to her and her people. She sat down on a moss-covered rock and watched as the clear water from the spring joined with the flowing water of the creek. She seemed to be mesmerized, comparing the lives of her people with the little stream. The water looked the same as it flowed by, but it was changing just as her people were.

Little Flower was startled when she heard her name called but was relieved when she turned to see Badger standing behind her. True to his word, he had not spoken of his feelings for her since he had promised to honor her wishes. She knew he watched over her and still spent time with her children. "Oh, Badger, you startled me," Little Flower said. "I did not know you were here."

"Little Flower, I will always be here," Badger smiled, "At least until you tell me to go away."

"Badger, you know that I," Little Flower began.

Badger placed his finger to her lips to silence her. "Little Flower, I know your feelings. I do not intend to say the words that you do not," he paused, "are not, ready to hear me say. I saw you come here. You looked so sad and unhappy. I wanted to make sure that you are well and that you do not need my help." Badger finished, noticing the tears that formed in her beautiful eyes.

"Thank you, Badger," Little Flower replied. "I am well and I have no problems, except for the terrible loss I feel for my husband. I do not believe this will ever go away," pausing, "you know that I still believe that he will return to me, and I will wait for him."

"Yes," Badger said sadly. "I know. Come, the darkness is beginning to fall. You do not need to be here alone. Others have looked at you too. Little Flower, you must use caution. After the time of the Green Corn Ceremony, some may think you are fair game."

The two of them walked back to the village, each deep in their own thoughts. Little Flower thinking of her husband and Badger thinking of her.

Chapter Thirty-Six

The Coweta Village had been cleaned and all the old utensils had been broken and replaced with new. Fasting and purification had taken place. New fires had been started. Many long talks were endured. Animated dances had been enjoyed. The warriors all participated in the drinking of the accee and new corn had been eaten. The eight days of Busk ended and all misconduct and evil deeds, except for the taking of a life, were forgiven. This was the first Busk celebrated following the terrible battles and tremendous loss of life of so many Creek people. The hearts of the Horseshoe refugees were still heavy and they desperately needed the time of renewal. They understood much more so than their new Coweta families the great change that had taken place.

The people from the Tallapoosa River Valley had great difficulty accepting the constant presence of white men when they first arrive in Coweta Town. Many were traders and others were passing through on their way to one of the big white towns outside of the Creek Nation. More surprising to them, were the large number of Creek women who had taken for their husband, one of the white men. These same men seemed to be gaining more control in the lives of the people. The Horseshoe refugees noticed too that the Coweta people did not see this change or had already accepted this new way of life. Many of the Red Stick women talked of this as they did their work. They were grateful to the Coweta for taking them in and providing food and shelter, but none of them were prepared for these lifestyle changes.

The morning after the final day of Busk, Sunflower Woman, Little Flower, Spotted Fawn and several of the Red Stick women had gone to the small stream to cleanse their soiled clothing. The women all laughed as first one and then another sat down in the stream, the cool water cooling their skin. This was their leisure time away from the Coweta women who always seemed to find some chore for the women from the Horseshoe to do.

"My mother, am I wrong in thinking that we have more work to do here than we had at our own village," Little Flower asked as she scrubbed her skirts with sand from the bottom of the stream.

"My daughter, you are right. Our work load is heavy here and it does seem that some of the Coweta women like to sit and watch us," Sunflower Woman lamented.

One of the young women, who had been selected to live with a particularly ill-mannered woman quickly added, "I was struck across the face when I complained about being tired before the Busk Ceremony."

"Why have you not spoken of this," Sunflower Woman questioned.

"I was told not to speak of this mistreatment and I have not had the opportunity to do so," the woman said, putting her hand to her face, remembering the sharp slap she had received.

"I think when we have the opportunity, we should go back home," another of the Horseshoe women added. "I do not want to stay here."

Looking sad and suddenly older to Little Flower, Sunflower Woman began to speak. "Now is a good time to tell you this," she paused, trying to think of the best words to say to her daughter and her friends.

"Tell us what," Spotted Fawn asked, feeling a sense of dread wash over her as she looked at the woman she loved as a mother.

"To begin with, you all know we have no place to go. We have no village and we have no men to take care of us," Sunflower Woman paused, again looking at each of the women, "And, and, we cannot go. The sister of Sings Softly Woman is a good woman. She treats me with kindness and she has confided in me. While we are treated well," Sunflower Woman looked at the woman who had told of being struck, "We are really captives. We will not be allowed to leave. We also will be expected to do much work, while some of the Coweta women watch."

"We are slaves then," Little Flower asked, remembering how some had been treated at her own village of Hillabee. "Why were we not told the truth?"

"We will have food and shelter and be allowed some free time. I was told we will not be treated cruelly. I will speak of the mistreatment that has occurred. This status will not change," pausing again, Sun Flower Woman continued, "Unless the Coweta warriors choose some of you to be their wives and then, in most cases, you would answer to their other wives. This is apparently the way it will be."

Silently the women spread their wet clothing on the rocks that lined the creek to dry. All of them were in a quiet, somber mood. The gay laughter they shared earlier had vanished. The woman who had said they should leave spoke again. "I will not stay here. I will not be treated in such a way. My father was the Hillabee Chief before the fighting began. I will be a slave to no one. I will watch and be ready. The opportunity for me to leave will come," She finished defiantly.

"My child," Sunflower Woman said, "You must not attempt this. You would not survive and if you were caught, things would only be worse. You cannot go back."

"My mother," Little Flower began, suddenly being filled with such a courageous spirit that could have only come from the grandmothers, "I too will not live my life here and neither will you. We are not slaves. I feel in my heart that we will be rescued."

"You do not need to be a slave," One of the others said. "We all know that the one called Badger would gladly make you his wife."

"I have a husband," Little Flower said, "And he will come for me."

"Little Flower," Spotted Fawn said quickly, "You know that Soaring Eagle, just as my husband, your brother Brave Hawk is gone. He will not come for you."

Spirit of the Red Stick Women

"You are wrong. Soaring Eagle still lives and he will come," Little Flower emphatically replied. "You can marry Badger if you like. He is a good man and will provide well for you. I will not become the wife of him or any other man. That is all I will say." Little Flower angrily grabbed her clean clothing and ran back up the path to Coweta Town. She had unfinished chores to do.

****

Chapter Thirty-Seven

Soaring Eagle and his people had wandered from village to village in the upper regions of Seminole country during the planting and hot season. Many times, they had been hungry before arriving at the next little village. Food was shared, shelter was offered and occasionally two or three women would stay with a Seminole Clan family. A few of the young warriors they encountered had traveled back to Pensacola Town to join with Peter McQueen. His own time in the frontier town was shortened when the Spanish Governor told him the food supply was extremely low and he did not expect to receive any more help. In fact, the Governor had also received word that the white soldiers including Sharp Knife Jackson were coming their way.

Soaring Eagle noticed that some of the women had trouble keeping up. Thinking they were fatigued from the long stretch of walking and the extreme heat, he ordered the group to stop under a grove of live oak trees. He was surprised to see a few of them lie down immediately.

"Grandmothers," Soaring Eagle asked, "What is wrong, why do you lie down?" As he drew closer to the women and several small children, he noticed the ugly red spots that covered their faces and arms. "Oh, no," He gasped, as he began backing away from the sickened victims. Was it measles or the dreaded pox? He could not take any chance. He quickly moved away from the infected group. Calling for the old medicine man, he counted five women and four children, all of them moaning in discomfort and pain.

After taking one look at them, the medicine man asked for water and for a fire to be made. He turned away and was quickly out of site as he began gathering leaves and berries from the bear grass that grew along the path.

Spirit of the Red Stick Women

Soaring Eagle had no idea where they were or how far they were from the nearest village. Villages had become fewer and farther apart and his food supply would only last a day or two at most. They most likely would not be allowed anywhere near a village. Once again, they were on their own. Fortunately, they had just forded a small creek. He knew they would have water and possibly small fish for food. He would send the older children to search for berries and any eatable plants they could find. He realized the big question now might not be of food, but what kind of sickness they were dealing with and how many more would be sick, or even die. Would this mean more burials for his people?

Taking a deep breath and praying to the Great Spirit that he did not come down with the sickness, Soaring Eagle walked up the path where the remainder of his people waited. They would need to know.

"My friends, there are words I need to tell you," Soaring Eagle said, looking at the forlorn group in front of him, their clothing tattered and some without moccasins. In each face, he saw the sorrow and grief that he himself felt. "Some of our people have," not knowing what the illness really was, he paused, "Are sick. Some have red spots and their bodies are hot."

"The pox, oh no," One woman almost screamed as she looked at her own arm. All of them started moving farther away.

"Let us not panic. We do not know yet what the sickness is. I want all of you to go and make camp in that next grove of trees," Soaring Eagle said pointing in the direction of trees he hoped would be far enough away from the sick. "You need rest and food. You know what to do. Do not come back to this place unless there is an emergency. I will stay and help our medicine man."

The Red Stick women and children began rapidly walking in the direction they were told to go. Whispering among themselves and asking the Great Spirit to protect them from the sickness.

After looking around the group, one of the women commented aloud to the woman beside her, "All of the sick are from one of the last towns, were we stopped. Soaring Eagle should not have allowed them to come with us. We have made it this far without any sickness."

"Our leader did not know they were sick and remember they asked to come with us to the River of Flowered Rocks where they have clan members who will take care of them," the other woman replied. "They are like us and we are like them. Neither of us have villages or men to take care of us."

"You are right. That was not good for me to say. I am tired and," pausing she continued, "And frightened. I just want to go home, not to some unfamiliar town where we do not know what our treatment will be," the first woman agreed.

"I too am afraid. Do not forget we are Red Stick women and the spirit of the grandmothers will see us through this. Come, let us do as we were told," the second woman said, forcing a smile and stooping to pick a handful of black berries from a scrubby vine growing beside the path.

Chapter Thirty-Eight

The old medicine man had gathered bear grass while Soaring Eagle built a fire and heated water. The sickened women and children drank the concoction, which immediately came back up. They were told to drink more slowly. This time they were able to keep the medicine down and drifted into a fitful sleep.

"What is the sickness," Soaring Eagle asked concerned. "Will it spread to others?"

"I not know for certain. I not think it pox. Women and children bad tired and weak. You need go to water and wash with honey locust leaves so sickness not cover you," The old man said as he looked at each of his patients. "Not know if they see sun of new day."

"Is it that bad," Soaring Eagle asked, frowning.

"Not know all about sickness of white man. Do all I can do," the old man said, sitting down, his back resting on one of the big oak trees. "Need for you to bring more water then go to others. I will keep heat from them," He said, pointing to the circle of sleeping women and children.

Soaring Eagle went to the stream and vigorously scrubbed himself with the leaves from the honey locust tree. Finding a place deep enough to submerge himself he relaxed, letting the cool water renew his strength. He did not realize how fatigued he was physically and how emotionally drained he had become. He found the need to seek the solace of the Great Spirit and decided that after making sure his people were settled, he would go deep into the woods and find the comfort and renewal he needed to continue.

The strength and spirit of the people he called his continued to amaze him. When he reached the grove of trees, he noticed the thin line of smoke as it curled into the air. He smelled the comforting scent of sofkee. His people, now numbering thirty-six, had prepared their meal and made a secure place to sleep. He told them of the still unknown sickness of the latest group to join with them. Reminding them, if they felt unwell to move away from the others. Soaring Eagle spoke softly with the three old warriors who remained, telling them of his plans.

"My brothers, I feel the need to renew myself with the Great Spirit. I will go to a place deep in that wooded area," Soaring Eagle pointed in the direction he intended to go. "I will ask for the strength and wisdom I will need to lead our people. If I am needed, do not hesitate to come for me, otherwise I will return with the new sun," The fatigued warrior said as he declined the offer of the fragrant sofkee.

Soaring Eagle walked into the deep woods of oak and pine trees. Following the worn trail of the deer, he soon spotted a small clearing near the little stream. A carpet of pine needles covered the forest floor. The full face of brother moon was beginning to shine, giving light to the darkness that had begun to settle over the woods. The evening birds and tree frogs began, as if on cue, their audible rituals for the coming night. Soaring Eagle quickly made a fire, to keep the big cats that roamed the area away more than to keep warm or to see.

He then went to the stream, thinking it best not to submerge himself again as he had noticed that brother snake grew quite large here. He kneeled and splashed the cold water over his face and chest, feeling the cold wash over him. He was ready now to commune with the Great Spirit and the world he had created.

Sitting down against the largest of the oak trees that surrounded the opening, Soaring Eagle realized that this was not the traditional way. There was no lodge for him to sweat and he had not gone the normal time without food or drink. He was still extremely hungry, forcing himself not to think of the sofkee he had refused earlier.

The night sounds soothed him, making him drowsy. His head dropped to his chest. He slept. He dreamed he heard the loud sounds of the big guns. He heard the cries of battle and saw warriors falling all around him. He saw the blood of his friend as he fell to the ground. He felt the sting of the knife as it entered his stomach and the force from the butt of a musket crashing down on his head. Soaring Eagle was suddenly awakened from his tormenting dreams by the chilling cry of the cat. Jumping to his feet, he grabbed his old musket, knowing he had very few lead balls remaining.

He did not need to use even one, unless it was absolutely necessary. The yellow eyes of the big black panther glared at him from across the nearly extinguished fire. Soaring Eagle could feel the cold sweat run down his face as he fumbled in his pouch for one of the balls. This was necessary. The big cat continued to look at him and slowly stepped forward. Just as Soaring Eagle took aim and was ready to pull the trigger, the cat gave another blood-curdling scream and then turned and leaped back into the darkness.

Taking a deep breath, Soaring Eagle put his musket down and rekindled the fire. He knew it was not the will of the Great Spirit for him to die. The cat could have killed him in mere seconds. Moistening his lips to fight his thirst, Soaring Eagle sat back down against the tree. Brother moon was directly overhead, now casting silvery light around the shaken warrior. "Great Spirit, maker of breath," He said aloud. "Thank you for sparing my life. I know now that you have purpose for me. Give me strength and guide the way for me so that I can help my people."

He sat very still, listening to the quieter sounds of the night, soon giving in once again to sleep. His dreams soon returned. This time he saw his children, their eyes dancing with excitement as they ran to him. Both talking at once, telling him of some great adventure. His daughter always trying to outdo her twin brother. Then he saw her, Little Flower, his beautiful flower, smiling at him, holding out her arms for him, "Come", she invited, "Come for me." In his dream, Soaring Eagle began to run to her, only to see her vanish. Then he heard the owl, the chilling cry of the owl.

Soaring Eagle cried out in his sleep, awaking himself. It was real, the sound of the owl was real. Loud at first, coming from the tree just over his head, then sailing to another, perching on a lower branch. Suddenly the owl flew, his cry soft and melancholy.

Soaring Eagle watched as if in a trance as the glowing embers of the fire slowly died away. He sat motionless as the quiet still of the pre-dawn closed over him. The sky turned from gray to pink and the woods around him began to come to life. He jumped as morning dew dripped from the tree on to his face and he watched as the first rays of the sun moved over the horizon. Feeling the weakness leave his body, he felt the renewed strength he had hoped for. He understood now. The Great Spirit had spared his life the night before. He had dreamed of the horrors of the Horseshoe and the sweetness of his family. The owl had returned with his chilling cry only to leave, taking the sadness with him. Soaring Eagle knew the Great Spirit would lead him and his people would survive.

Chapter Thirty-Nine

After taking the time to refresh himself in the steam and to eat, a handful of ripened blackberries, Soaring Eagle went first to check on the condition of the sick women and children. He found the old medicine man bathing the face of one of the older women, then urging her to drink hot liquid from a clay cup. Looking around he counted four women and three children. All of them were sitting up and appeared to be better. Looking at the medicine man, Soaring Eagle asked the question, fearing that he already knew the answer. "Where are?"

The old man shook his head. "They too weak. Need your help to bury later. The sickness is not pox and others," smiling, he said, "And this old woman will live."

"That is good," Soaring Eagle said. "I will go now to see about my people, then return to help you."

"Yes, I need food for the sick and myself. Then we will go do unpleasant task," pausing the old medicine man looked intently at the young warrior, "Soaring Eagle, you find what you seek? Did Great Spirit show you way for future?"

"Yes, the Great Spirit will guide me. I will tell you what I saw during the time of brother moon," Soaring Eagle answered.

"About big cat and owl," the medicine man asked.

"You know," Soaring inquired, confused.

A smile covered the old wrinkled face of the medicine man as he turned back to the old woman, assuring her that she would live.

Soaring Eagle walked briskly toward the grove of trees where his people waited anxiously for his return. He knew by the smoke that the morning meal was being prepared and he hoped all was well. Several of the children ran to meet him as he entered the little make-shift camp. Missing his own son and daughter, Soaring Eagle was quick to show kindness to the little ones. Seeing the actions of the children, one of the old warriors made his way slowly to their leader.

"Soaring Eagle, are you well this new day? What of the sick," the aged man asked, rubbing his legs as if to make them move better.

"Yes, all is well with me this day. It is with much sorrow that I tell you that one of the older women and the youngest child did not live to see the new sun. The sickness is leaving the others and they will recover. The sickness is not pox," Soaring Eagle said, seeing the relief in the old face. "My people here, are they still well?"

"Yes, no one is sick. We have fish and fresh sofkee. You eat now," The old man said.

"Yes, I will eat and take food back to the others," Soaring Eagle said, taking the food offered to him. "We will need to stay here until the sick are strong enough to travel. Can you find food to last for two or three more suns?"

"Plenty fish in little stream. Women find berries. We will have food," the old warrior answered, happy to be able to help his leader.

"That is good. I will go back to the sick now," Soaring Eagle stated.

Soaring Eagle returned to the camp of the sick. After giving them food, he and the medicine man attended to the unpleasant task of burying the woman and child, a little girl who had enjoyed so little life. He could feel the tears welling in his eyes as he gently wrapped the child in a worn blanket. Not having real tobacco, the medicine man sparingly sprinkled sumac leaves over the still bodies. They were then buried in a shallow grave as others before them had been and more would be in the future. After completing the burial and making sure the sick were resting comfortably, the old medicine man touched Soaring Eagle on the shoulder and said, "Come, walk with me."

The two men, decades apart in age, had become close friends, each respecting the other's wisdom and ability. They walked in silence, the morning sun beating down on their dark faces. Soaring Eagle was the first to speak. "Tell me how you knew of the cat and the owl?"

"My son, it not big mystery," the old man laughed. "I hear cry of both. I know already you get their visit and that Great Spirit show way for you to follow. Are you willing to do what expected of you,' he asked, knowing how the young leader would answer?

"I am willing. I need to find my family before I can lead my people. Will you help me," the young warrior asked?

"We will find your family. The Great Spirit come to me in dream, my son. The time ahead for you and our people will not be easy. Many of our warriors have died in battle. Most of our towns no longer here. Our women and children wander from place to place. Many taken to towns of other people. Some not treated good," the old man paused, gazing out at the tree-lined meadow as if seeing into the future. "There will be good time again. Our people think bad time over. It will come again. More, many more people with white skin come. They not want to trade for deer skin. They want more. They want our land. The white man take Creek land," the old medicine man paused again, tears streaming down his wrinkled face. "Make our people move away to new place. Many Indian people die on path. Time bad, very bad for long time."

Soaring Eagle and the old medicine man sat, neither aware of the hot sun beaming down on them or of the cheerful singing of the wren and bluebirds that flittered around them. Both men were deep in thought, one thinking of his past and the other of his future.

Soaring Eagle had hoped to be back on the path in two suns and surely the River of Flowered Rocks could not be much farther away. Once there he hoped the journey would be easier. He realized the travel to the north, to Coweta Town, would still be far. He so desperately wanted to see his Little Flower and the children. The heart-sick warrior did not know that the heat of the growing season would turn into the cold time of falling leaves and he would still be in search of his family.

****

Chapter Forty

Red Fox and Little Deer sat quietly behind the bushes that bordered the village. They listened as two men, one white, the other brown talked, their voices becoming louder in anger.

"You will pay me for the rum and the shroud cloth or else," the white trader said, pulling his vest closer to his chest.

"I have no coin of white man. I say to you before you give firewater and blanket, we trade. I give skin of deer. Make good leggings for you," the young Creek warrior answered.

"I have no need for this skin. I demand my payment. You said you could pay me," the trader continued to yell, his face turning red.

"What I pay with," the Creek innocently asked?

"I will take none of this impudence from you. You red heathen," the trader smirked as he pulled a loaded pistol from his trouser pocket and pointed it at the startled young man.

Reacting with swiftness, the young warrior pulled his knife from his belt. His aim was accurate. The white man looked down at his stomach as red stained his fancy vest. He dropped the gun and he fell to the ground.

A sense of dread filled the young warrior, remembering only three suns before, a drunken Creek man had been hung for killing a trader. He did not know if this man was dead or not. He could not wait to see. He was in trouble. He pulled the knife from the man and turned to leave before anyone noticed what had happened. Tripping as he turned, he looked down seeing two wide-eyed children looking up at him.

"What," he softly said as he looked over his shoulder, glad to see that the incident had not yet been detected. "Who are you, why are you here?" Not knowing what to do about the children who had apparently witnessed the possible murder, the warrior grabbed each child by the hand and pulled them with him. "You come with me now," he ordered.

Both children began kicking and screaming. Being so far from the village no one had heard. The warrior walked as fast as he could, forcing the children to run to keep up. When he noticed, the children were gasping for breath, he stopped.

Neither child showed the fear they felt. Instead, both glared at the warrior. Looking again over his shoulder, he stared back at them. "Again, I ask what were you doing back there? What did you see? Who are you," he insisted.

In a surprisingly calm voice, the little girl answered, "I am Little Deer, this is my brother Red Fox. We were going to gather acorns for our mother. We saw the white man with the big stomach point his gun at you."

"It is good you were fast with your knife," the boy chimed in. "He had his finger on his trigger. Tell us your name and why did you make us come with you?"

Feeling as if he were being interrogated, the young warrior, who was not many seasons older than the children, smiled slightly and said, "I see you have no fear, that is good. I was called Boy Who Steals Horse. Now, "standing straighter, he continued," I am Horse Stealer."

"Why do you run," Little Deer asked, her eyes shining brightly.

"I think I killed that man. Under the white man law, I will hang for that," Horse Stealer said looking back in the direction of the village. "I am not ready to die."

"Where will you go," Red Fox asked, taking an immediate liking to their captor.

"Down river, I have clan members in a town there. They will hide us," Horse Stealer said, urging the children to start moving again.

"Us, why do we need to go? We did nothing," Little Deer asked, showing fear for the first time.

"You saw what I did. They will make you talk. Now come. I will not hurt you," Horse Stealer promised.

"We do not want," Little Deer began, only to be silenced by the young warrior.

"You will come with me. That is all," Horse Stealer demanded. Grabbing the arms of the children, the three began walking again at a quick pace. The sun was directly overhead before they stopped to drink water from a cool spring that dripped from the rocks.

The children had been quiet as they walked, realizing they had been taken captive. While they did not think Horse Stealer would hurt them, they wanted to be with their mother and the safety of what they considered their temporary home. Little Deer, wiping the water from her mouth, looked up at the young warrior. He could see that she was trying hard not to cry as she softly spoke. "Please let us go. We will not tell of what we saw."

"Yes, we will promise not to talk," Red Fox added, feeling protective of his sister. We will say, we strayed too far from the village while we were looking for nuts. No one will ever know we saw you."

"I am sorry," Horse Stealer said, regretting that he had made the children come with him. "You have been gone too long. If anyone is looking for me, they will connect my absence with you."

"What do you intend to do with us," Red Fox asked, "You cannot keep us with you until we become a man and a woman."

Smiling the young warrior answered, "No, I do not want that. Let me think. We will be at the town of my clan members before the sun leaves the sky, if we walk fast. Then I will decide. Come, let us continue on."

"Will this town be filled with the white people like Coweta Town," Little Deer asked, hoping there would be no white-skinned people at all. She was uncomfortable in their presence.

"No, it is a small town. Some of the warriors actually fought with the Red Sticks," Horse Stealer answered. "What is the name of your father and mother?"

Spirit of the Red Stick Women

"Our mother is Little Flower," Little Deer said quickly, and …

Speaking before his sister could finish, Red Fox proudly added, "and our father is Soaring Eagle, Micco of the Hillabee on the Tallapoosa. Badger said he was killed at the Horseshoe."

Not allowing her brother to continue, the little girl said happily, "Our mother says he still lives and he will come for us."

Looking stunned, Horse Stealer took a deep breath. He had heard of the prowess of Soaring Eagle. He knew of the quiet strength of Badger and that he considered the beautiful Little Flower to be his, threatening to kill anyone who touched her.

"Oh, I am in deep trouble," Horse Stealer whispered. "We will still continue down river. Before the sun is low in the new day, I will have someone get you back to Coweta Town." Sounding as stern as he could, he continued, "Both of you must promise me that you will say you wandered off and got lost," the young warrior finished, fearing the consequences of his actions, "And not a word of what you saw."

Chapter Forty-One

Children, on the pretense of gathering nuts, often played in the woods for hours and were not missed. On this day, the twins had not been missed. As Sunflower Woman helped her daughter prepare the midday meal for the twins, she began to wonder where her grandchildren were. "Little Flower, did the children mention what they would do this day," the older woman asked? "It is not like them to be gone for so long.

"Red Fox said he and his sister were going into the woods to gather nuts. That was just after they had finished their morning sofkee," Little Flower answered her mother. "They may be playing with other children and not realize how long they have been gone."

Frowning, the Sunflower Woman remarked to her daughter, as she bent to turn the bread of corn that sizzled in the iron pan. "It is easier to cook bread like this, but I enjoyed cooking the old way. Our food taste better then. Maybe the children are playing and will be back soon, I just have this feeling that something is not right."

Just as Sunflower Woman finished speaking, they heard a loud commotion coming from the town square. Having only suffered a flesh wound, the trader was more infuriated that a young warrior would dare attempt to kill him. No matter that his pistol was still by his side when the others had rushed to his aid. His loud curses were heard proclaiming the guilt of the one called Horse Stealer.

"He took my goods and then tried to kill me. I demand that he be apprehended and dealt with," the irate trader shouted.

Recognizing the trader as being the newest of many to ply their wares at Coweta, most of the town people soon went back to the activities they had been involved in before the interruption. This particular trader, with his fancy vest, had earned no respect. Only some of the other traders and a few white men with their own interest in mind stayed to listen to his rants, while his wound was attended to.

"I say we go after this thief," one of the men said, having found life in the Creek town to be quite dull, "I could use some action."

"Yes, I agree. When we find him, we will make him pay," another man said, laughing.

Sunflower Woman and Little Flower had heard the remarks of the men. Both mother and grandmother became more concerned when the other women reported they had not seen the twins and that their children were all at their huti doing chores. The twins seemed to find a way to put themselves in danger.

Badger had just returned from a hunt and had heard some of the commotion. He dropped the deer he had killed at the huti of his mother and moved toward the square ground.

"What is going on here," the concerned warrior asked, looking at the trader who was screaming like a child.

"I have been robbed and the thieving red heathen tried to kill me," the trader yelled again as the stab wound was covered with moss. He realized he had a new audience and used the opportunity to act as if his injury was more severe.

Covering his mouth to hide his smile Badger answered him. "It is not so bad. What was taken from you. Do you know who the man is?"

"He called himself Horse Stealer," the trader said, still pretending to be in pain. "He took some of my whiskey and a fine piece of red shroud."

"Horse Stealer, he is barely more than a child. Did he give you anything in return?" Badger asked suspiciously?

"Well, yes, he gave me a deer hide. It was not a fair trade. When I asked for coins, he laughed at me and threw his knife," pointing to his blood-soaked shirt he continued, "See it went right into my stomach. I demand justice."

Guessing there was more to the story, Badger continued the interrogation. "And then what happened?"

"I saw him turn and walk away as I fell to the ground," the devious trader replied, not saying that he thought he had fainted. "He seemed to trip. He was talking to someone. I think it was children. That is all I remember. Are you going after him?"

"Yes, yes, I will," Badger said as he turned, bumping into Little Flower. "Little Flower, what are you doing here?" the startled man asked.

"Red Fox and Little Deer, they are gone," the young woman said with fear in her voice. "I heard what this man said. Do you think my children are with the young warrior?"

Shaking his head in disbelief at what these children could get into, Badger answered as he grabbed her and pulled her away from the prying eyes of the trader. "It is possible. How long have the children been missing?"

Little Flower told Badger that the children had gone into the woods to hunt for nuts earlier that morning. When they had not returned, she and her mother had searched the town and no one had seen the children. She did not think they would stay gone for so long without good reason.

"That is true. If they are with Horse Stealer they will be safe. He will not harm them," Badger promised, beginning to fear for the children himself. "I will go in search of them as soon as I see my mother."

"I too will go," Little Flower answered, tears forming in her eyes. "They are my children."

"Little Flower," Badger began, "Please stay here with Sunflower Woman."

"No. I will go." The beautiful woman said.

Badger looked at her, knowing of her strong will and also knowing he loved her more than ever. "As you wish, come," he said.

Chapter Forty-Two

The bright sun quickly dropped behind the leafless trees and the cool of the upcoming night chilled the air.

"I am cold," the small voice of the little girl broke the silence.

"And I am hungry," her brother added. "There will soon be no light to see. Will we stop and make fire and try to find food?"

The child was smart, too smart. Horse Stealer thought to himself, wishing again that he had not taken the children. He could walk all night and be at Sauwoogalooche Town by the time the sun rose. He knew the children could not. The trip was taking longer than he had expected. He had not intended to be so abrupt. It was not the fault of these children that they were here.

"The two of you look for small sticks while we walk. There is a good spot to make camp up the path. We will need to make do with nuts if I cannot find a rabbit to kill," the young warrior answered. Luckily as he finished speaking a large rabbit ran in front of them. In a flash, the knife of Horse Stealer extended from the animal.

"The aim of Horse Stealer is good," Red Fox said admiringly.

"If you can skin the animal, I will build a fire," Horse Stealer said. "Little Deer, you search for nuts and we will eat."

"Yes", both children said, beginning to enjoy the adventure.

Soon the three sat in front of the fire, enjoying the warmth and the tasty rabbit. Licking his fingers, Red Fox broke the silence. "Will you stay in Sauwoogalooche Town? Will the mean old trader come looking for you?"

Before Horse Stealer could answer, Little Deer promptly asked, "Do you have a mother there, or a wife?"

"Do you children always ask so many questions?" the young warrior laughed. "Yes, I will stay in Sauwoogaloochee.

Spirit of the Red Stick Women

It is a safe town and the trader cannot harm me there, and I do have family. I need for the two of you to say nothing to anyone when we arrive. Let me explain. Do you understand?"

"Yes, we understand, "the twins said again in unison.

"You even speak at the same time," Horse Stealer laughed again. "Now, both of you go lie on that pile of straw. We have no blankets. I will try to keep the fire burning." A coyote howled off in a distance as he finished speaking, "To keep brother coyote away. We will be moving again when the sun shows her face. We will have morning sofkee at my town."

Chapter Forty-Three

Badger and Little Flower left Coweta Town immediately, thinking the children and Horse Stealer, if they were with him, could not have traveled for. Badger guessed that they would go to Sauwoogalooche. He did not know that Horse Stealer had purposely taken an alternate route instead of going directly to the town.

Walking at a fast pace, they quickly covered a long distance and had not seen any sign of the children. Both had walked in silence, deep in thought. Badger noticed that Little Flower seemed to be tiring.

"Little Flower, we need to rest briefly before continuing," Badger said. "We will stop at that little stream up ahead."

"Badger, I am not stopping to rest until I find my children," the determined woman replied.

"Little Flower, we will find the children, but we need to rest and drink water," Badger urged. "We will stop."

"Yes, Badger, I am sorry to give you so much trouble," Little Flower answered. "I fear for my children. They seem to find danger."

"Yes, they do. If they are with Horse Stealer, and I think they are, they will be safe. We will find them, even if we have to go all the way to Sauwoogalooche," Badger promised.

"Thank you, Badger," Little Flower said as she cupped water from the stream into her small hands.

They continued to walk as the sun sank lower in the sky, soon finding themselves with the same dilemma as the children and Horse Stealer. Not taking the time to secure food or warm clothing, Badger and Little Flower would need to do the same as Horse Stealer had done. Badger quickly built a fire and Little Flower managed to catch two small fish from the stream. They ate in silence, Badger watching Little Flower intently. He knew she was trying to be brave and not give into the fear she felt. He saw the tears glisten in her beautiful eyes as the firelight twinkled in the darkness.

"It will be cold later. You will need to stay close to the fire to be warm," Badger said, wishing he could hold her close to provide warmth.

Stars blinked in the night sky and the face of brother moon soon rose over the horizon. Sounds of the night filled the crisp air. Her head nodding, Little Flower slowly succumbed to the fear and fatigue of the day. Badger watched as she inched closer to the fire and lay down on the sage brush he had gathered for her. He looked around for something to cover her with. Seeing nothing, he also succumbed to his wishes and lay down beside her. Their bodies only slightly touching. She shivered and he put his arm around her and pulled her closer. Both slipped into a deep sleep.

Little Flower awoke to the howl of a prowling coyote and was startled to find herself in the arms of Badger, the strong warrior gazing intently at the beautiful woman.

Little Flower screamed, "Badger, what are you doing? Why are you so close to me," she questioned as she freed herself from his arms.

"It is cold Little Flower; the fire does not give enough heat. I'm only trying to keep you warm," Badger answered, seemingly embarrassed.

"Please move away," the alarmed woman said.

"Little Flower, look at me," Badger said, lifting her face to his. "I love you."

Little Flower turned away. "Badger, stop. Do not do this to yourself. You know that my heart belongs to Soaring Eagle. Please find another to give your love."

Sitting up and placing more sticks on the dying fire, Badger angrily answered, "Little Flower, why can you not understand that Soaring Eagle does not live. You are free to love again."

"Badger, again I tell you that you are a brave warrior and I know you would make me a good husband. My love, my Eagle, is coming for me and I know it will be soon," Little Flower said tenderly, reaching out to touch his face. "I cannot love you."

Neither slept again. Both sat watching the glowing fire and listening to the coyotes and the distant sound of the owl. The owl no longer frightening, but sad and melancholy.

****

Chapter Forty-Four

Soaring Eagle and his forlorn group of travelers had encountered hardship after hardship. Many had suffered from sickness, taking days at a time to recover. Many more were old and tired and could only walk a short distance each day. One young woman had given birth to a child, the tiny little one crying to his death because his mother had no milk to provide for his nourishment.

Only five or six had stayed at one of the few towns they had come across. Most of his people had no one else and would go with Soaring Eagle wherever he had to go. They had reached the waters of the river called Flowered Rocks and began their trip to the north. Towns were more numerous and food more plentiful. For the first time in many moons no one was hungry. This was good and the hearts of the people became lighter and laughter could be heard from the younger ones. Soaring Eagle was told that Coweta Town could be reached in three suns if his people could move at a normal pace. He was also told that Coweta was a White Stick, peace town and that many white people were living either in the town or nearby. A Red Stick Warrior would not be welcome there and his life would be in danger.

Dejected and saddened, Soaring Eagle sat by the river watching the white rapids form over the rocks as the water raced by. He did not notice the old medicine man until he had stiffly sat down by the young micco.

"Soaring Eagle, my son," the old man said. "What plans do you have to retrieve your family? One old man tell me some of our people from Horseshoe slaves there. May not let them go."

"I do not know," the young micco answered. "I will get my family and all of our people, somehow."

"Yes, I see in dream, you will get our people. I see us back on Tallapoosa," the wise old medicine man said softly.

****

Chapter Forty-Five

Horse Stealer and the children were on the path before the first rays of sun streaked the gray sky. The children had given their captor no more trouble and did as they were told. He was beginning to grow fond of the children and knew he would miss their constant questions.

Morning activities of the town were soon heard and the smell of cooking meat drifted through the air, making the twins and Horse Stealer hungry. All three of them quickened their step and soon came inside the bustling town. Several children, about the age of the twins, and two large gray dogs ran to greet the visitors.

"Horse Stealer, uncle, it is good to see you," one of the little boys said. "Are you coming home now? Who are they?" he asked, staring at Red Fox and Little Deer.

"Gray Rabbit, it is good to see you too," Horse Stealer answered, lifting the son of his sister high in the air. "I am here for a visit and these are my new little friends." Sniffing the air, Horse Stealer smiled, "Could my sister be roasting meat? We are hungry."

"My mother has much good meat. Come," the little boy said importantly.

Several people greeted Horse Stealer as he and the children walked through the town. He was well-liked and had many friends. Seeing him, Singing Basket rushed to hug her younger brother, asking him the same questions her son had.

"My sister, I do not know how long my stay will be," Horse Stealer said pointing to Red Fox and Little Deer. "These children are from the Horseshoe and should return to Coweta Town as soon as arrangements can be made."

"From the Horseshoe," Singing Basket asked, surprised. "What are they doing with you?"

Spirit of the Red Stick Women

"It is a very complicated story. One that I will talk of when we are alone," the young warrior said, indicating he would say no more.

Understanding the meaning of the words of her brother, Singing Basket swiftly cut sizzling meat from the deer hanging over the fire and poured fresh sofkee into bowls for the children and her brother. "Come, sit children. You must be very hungry and tired. You must rest," Singing Basket said in a motherly way, realizing the children had to be nervous and frightened. "What are your names?"

"I am Little Deer and this is my brother, Red Fox," the Little girl replied bravely. "Our home is," pausing, she continued, "Was, Hillabee Town on the Oakfuskee River."

"And our father is Soaring Eagle. He is the micco," the little boy proudly added. "He is coming for us."

Singing Basket gave her brother a puzzled, inquiring look as she handed him his food. Having heard of the terrible destruction of the Tallapoosa town and that most of the Red Sticks at the Horseshoe had been killed, she wondered if these children were orphans. Not knowing how to respond to the information the children had freely given her, Singing Basket smiled and patted each child on the head. "You eat now."

Horse Stealer finished his food and gave instructions to Gray Rabbit to stay with the children. He motioned for his sister to follow him. He knew she would know best what he should do. He quickly and quietly revealed to her the predicament he had created.

"Oh, Horse Stealer," the older sister said. "You are in bad trouble. Are you sure the trader is dead?"

"I do not know. He was on the ground and I saw blood when I pulled my knife from his stomach," Horse Steal said as he rubbed his aching head.

"Why did you take the children? This only makes matters worse," Singing Basket anxiously stated.

"I told you, they saw what I did. I know that I was wrong. I did not think. Oh, Singing Basket, what will I do," the young warrior exclaimed.

"I will think of something. We will get the children back to their mother as quickly as we can. That will solve one problem. It will be good if the trader is not dead." Seeing the dread in the eyes of her younger brother, she continued, "Do not worry."

Chapter Forty-Six

As the two walked back to the huti of Singing Basket, they heard sounds of excitement coming from the lower side of the town. The curious group of on-lookers parted as a weary group of mostly women and children led by a fatigued, but impressive warrior and a few old men entered the square ground.

The townspeople stood in small groups talking among themselves, all wondering who the strangers were. Little Deer and Red Fox, as always, were inquisitive and had followed the group of people. Being too short to see, the children stood and waited. In the silence before their father began speaking, the eyes of the children locked. Red Fox reached out and took his sister's hand. They heard the voice they had not heard in many moons, one they feared they would never hear again.

"I am Soaring Eagle, micco of the Hillabee. I come from the Horseshoe in search of my family," Soaring Eagle announced.

Both children began pushing and shoving the warriors and women. As if they understood the importance of this unusual behavior, the crowd parted. Red Fox and Little Deer, shouting as they ran, "My father, my father!"

Unashamed tears rolled down the face of the strong, brave warrior as his children jumped into his arms. "My children, Red Fox and my Little Deer. On, my children," the jubilant father cried.

"Our mother said you would come," Little Deer said, wiping tears from her eyes.

Expecting to see his wife emerge from the crowd, Soaring Eagle, disappointed when he did not see her, inquired, "Your mother, where is she?"

"She is with Badger. They are looking for us, I think," Red Fox said, smiling broadly at his father.

Spirit of the Red Stick Women

Not Badger again. Soaring Eagle thought to himself. "With Badger? Why is she with him and you are here," he asked, trying not to show the concern and anger he felt.

Horse Stealer stepped forward. "They came here with me," he nervously said in awe of the chieftain warrior who had survived the Horseshoe.

"Who are you and why do you have my children," Soaring Eagle demanded.

"I am Horse Stealer. My reason for having your children is complicated and my words will be long," hoping to break the tension that was beginning to form, he continued. "Please, tell your people they are welcome. We have food to share."

"Yes, thank you. My people are tired and we have had no food this day," Soaring Eagle said, motioning for the group behind him to come forward. "I will eat after I hear your words." Taking each child by the hand, he followed Horse Stealer to a private place where they could talk.

"Now, Horse Stealer," Soaring Eagle began, "Tell me why you have my children and why my wife is with this Badger."

Horse Stealer sensing that this heroic man was jealous, smiled, thinking that he had a good reason to be. "Your family was brought to Coweta Town," the young warrior began, only to be interrupted by Soaring Eagle.

"By Badger? He was at the Horseshoe, then" the glaring-eyed warrior angrily shouted.

"Yes," Horse Stealer answered, wiping the moisture from his forehead.

"I am sorry, please continue," Soaring Eagle said, regaining his composure.

"I had been at Coweta Town only a short time. I do not know the whole story. Your children can better tell you than I," Horse Stealer admitted, telling Soaring Eagle of his involvement, including the possibility of killing the trader. "And that is why I brought your children here. I would guess that your wife," pausing, "and Badger are somewhere between this town and Coweta. I am sorry to have included Red Fox and Little Deer in this situation. They are good children."

Understanding Horse Stealer did have a problem, Soaring Eagle smiled, realizing the young warrior had taken care of his children. "My children are smart and they do have a way of finding excitement and danger. I will have food and then I will go in search of my wife and this Badger. I am sure he will not be happy to see me." Smiling again he promised, "I will hold my wife in my arms before the sun sets on this day."

Horse Stealer suggested that he accompany Soaring Eagle. He knew the route that Badger would take to get to Sauwoogaloochee. He also knew there was a good chance there would be trouble when the two met. He respected both warriors and hoped that he might help to resolve the bad feelings between the two. The young warrior and the Hillabee Chieftain set out, Soaring Eagle assuring his children that he would return with their mother.

****

Chapter Forty-Seven

Badger and Little Flower said little to each other. She had refused the offer of food left from the night before, telling him she needed to find her children. Seeing the look of total rejection in his face, the beautiful woman sadly smiled at him, tears shining in her eyes. "Badger, I am sorry. You know that."

"Yes, I know. Say no more. Let us go now," the warrior said, furious at himself for allowing his emotions to show.

"Badger, I must tell you this. I dreamed of Soaring Eagle. I will be in his arms before the sun sets on this day," Little Flower said, having no idea her husband had voiced the same words.

Badger shook his head, "Come."

They moved in silence, hearing only the early morning sounds as the forest came to life. They walked rapidly and soon heard the gurgling sounds of a rock-filled stream.

"Little Flower, please use caution when crossing. The rocks are treacherous," Badger said as he stepped from stone to stone. He guessed correctly that she would refuse any assistance from him.

Badger had safely crossed and looked back just as Little Flower slipped, her foot catching on the last stone. The young woman fell forward, hitting her head on a large rock that jutted out near the edge of the bank.

"Little Flower," Badger shouted as he ran back to her. "Are you hurt?" He lifted her tiny body, seeing a trickle of blood run down her face.

"I am not hurt," Little Flower answered, rubbing her head. "If you will just put me down, I will wash the blood from my face and we can continue. I have only scratched my face on the sharp edge of the rock."

Badger placed Little Flower back on her feet, still concerned. He knew she had taken a nasty fall. Immediately sinking back to the ground, Little Flower grabbed her ankle. "Oh, I must have turned my ankle too."

Badger picked her up again and carried her away from the stream and sat her down on a moss-covered log. "Let me see. Be still Little Flower," he said as he rubbed his hands over her already swelling foot. "It is not broken, just bruised. You will not be able to walk very well. Let me help you back to the stream and you can soak your foot in the cold water. That will help the swelling to go down."

Badger saw the tears welling in her beautiful eyes, wanting again to hold her close he pleaded, "Little Flower, please do not cry anymore."

"I need to find my children," she sobbed, the tears streaking down her cheeks. "Now, I cannot walk!"

"We will find Red Fox and Little Deer. I will carry you if necessary. Just keep your foot in the water a little longer," Badger ordered.

"Yes, I will do as you say. Badger, I am so sorry. I have caused you much trouble," Little Flower softly answered, taking a deep breath. She watched impatiently as the cold water swirled past her ankle.

"I think we can go now. I found a firm stick to help with your balance," Badger said as he carefully helped her to her feet. "I will support you as we walk."

The two of them began to walk. The expression on Little Flowers face showed that she was in much pain and would indeed need the help of the strong warrior. Little Flower suddenly stopped. Badger, thinking that she needed more help moved closer, placing his arms around her.

"Soaring Eagle, she whispered. "He is here."

The Hillabee Chieftain stood on the path. Seeing his wife in the arms of another strong warrior, an uncontrollable rage consumed Soaring Eagle. The eyes of the two warriors locked, both knowing immediately the identity of the other. Badger was shocked and felt a great sadness wash over him. Soaring Eagle was the first to break the heavy silence.

"You are Badger. Release my wife, now or you will die," the furious warrior shouted as he pulled his knife from his belt.

"And you are Soaring Eagle. So, you do live," Badger answered calmly, showing no fear.

"Yes, I live. Do as I say or you will not," Soaring Eagle replied, letting his guard down as his eyes washed over the beautiful woman, his Little Flower. He had willed himself to live for this moment when he could see her again.

"I cannot," Badger answered, "If I …,

Rage raced through Soaring Eagle as he lunged toward Badger, knocking both the warrior and the woman to the ground. Badger jumped to his feet, reaching for his knife. Little Flower screamed as her husband approached, wild-eyed with his knife high in the air.

"Soaring Eagle, stop! Do not harm him, please," Little Flower begged.

Horse Stealer, stood behind Soaring Eagle, watching the scene unfold. Fearing that one or both would be severely injured or killed, he bravely leaped between the two men. Standing between them, he silently watched as each warrior seemingly analyzed the other. Soaring Eagle, regaining his composure, looked again at his wife. Tears formed in the eyes of the valiant warrior as he helped her to her feet.

"Little Flower, my flower," He whispered as she fell into his arms.

"My Eagle, I knew that you lived and that you would come for me," Little Flower responded.

The tender embrace they shared was so emotional that both Badger and Horse Stealer turned away, allowing the warrior and his wife their time of privacy.

Chapter Forty-Eight

Little Flower, pointing to her swollen ankle, fully explained to her husband why she had been in the arms of another warrior. Nodding his head, slightly embarrassed by his behavior, Soaring Eagle called out to Badger, "Come, we must have words."

The two warriors wearily eyed each other again, one feeling immense jubilation, the other tremendous sadness. This time, Badger broke the silence. "I am Badger. Obviously, you know of me," he paused, deciding to be honest with this man who had defied death and had walked for many moons to find the woman that he, too, loved. "I am from Coweta Town, I was at the Horseshoe. I was ordered to bring women and children to the River of Flowered Rocks."

At the mention of her children, Little Flower quietly asked, "My Children, where are my children?"

"They are at the town of Sauwoogalooche. They are safe," Horse Stealer said, feeling important. He realized that he had helped to defuse a potentially bad situation.

Smiling happily, Little Flower moved closer to her husband, who warmly placed his arm around her. Badger continued, "Soaring Eagle, I have brought your family to safety, keeping them from harm along the way," he paused and smiled, "and at times the antics of your children made it difficult."

The intense expression on Soaring Eagle's face softened as he thought of the twins and their strong-willed personality, "Yes," he nodded.

Choosing to leave nothing out, the Coweta warrior looked at Little Flower, the love he felt for her obvious in his eyes. "And you should know, that I have looked at the wife of Soaring Eagle."

The Hillabee Chieftain stiffened but said nothing.

Spirit of the Red Stick Women

"Thinking you could not have survived the ..." he paused, the vivid scene at the Horseshoe flashing before him, Badger softly continued, "The horrific battle. I then offered my love to Little Flower. She refused me," sadly smiling he finished, "She told me that you lived and that you would come for her. You are here. That is all," Badger said, his heart heavy. "There is one more thing you should know. I am sorry your people have suffered. I would have never gone to the Horseshoe if I had known the outcome."

The warriors looked at each other. Both seeming to search the soul of the other. Soaring Eagle nodded, "Thank you for protecting my family. I know others in your position would not have been as honorable." Feeling new respect for each other, the two firmly clasped the arm of the other.

Chapter Forty-Nine

Breathing a sigh of relief that her husband and Badger had resolved their problems, Little Flower sweetly asked, "Can we go to my children now?"

"Yes," Soaring Eagle said, "I have seen them, Little Flower. They are anxious for you and are ready for us to be reunited."

"That is good, but what of my mother and the others," Little Flower asked, remembering the situation of the people at Coweta Town.

"I will take you to the children and then go to get our people," Soaring Eagle said, unaware that it would not be so simple.

"No." Badger interjected, "You cannot go to Coweta Town. It is the home of General McIntosh. Do you forget that you are a Red Stick Warrior? You will be shot on site."

Remembering that he had been warned of this earlier, Soaring Eagle frowned, "What will I do then? My people should be with me."

"You and Little Flower return to Sauwoogalooche. I will go back to Coweta Town. Soaring Eagle, you should know that some of the people from the Horseshoe are," pausing not knowing how the Hillabee Chieftain would respond, "are slaves. They will not be returned to you."

Nodding his head again, "Yes, I have heard this too," looking at Little Flower he continued. "What of Sunflower Woman?"

"The sister of my mother has given her a home. She is not treated as a slave. I think I can secure her return as well as the wife of the brother of Little Flower and her children. The others, I do not know," Badger answered sadly.

"Is it safe for me to go with you," Horse Stealer asked.

"No, it is not," Badger answered.

"The trader, he did not live, then?" Horse Stealer asked again, fear covering his face.

"He still lives. He is an evil man and has said much untruth about you. If you return, you will be killed too," Badger said, looking at the young warrior.

"Go now, and take Soaring Eagle and Little Flower back to your town so they can be reunited with their children. I will go to Coweta Town. I do not know how much time it will take, but I will return with your family," Badger said, looking at Little Flower, the light of love still shining in his eyes.

"Thank you, Badger. You have done much for my family," the Hillabee Micco stated, aware of how Badger had looked at his wife.

Moving slowly and using the stick Badger had found for her, Little Flower limped over to the surprised warrior and lightly kissed him on the cheek. "For that I will always be grateful and remember this, I am sorry," the beautiful woman said, limping back to her husband's side. Soaring Eagle placed his arm around her again. Seeing the tears shining in her eyes, he realized that only by the grace of the Great Spirit, had he and his Little Flower been reunited.

"Soaring Eagle, where will you and your family go? I have heard the white soldiers still roam the Creek land. There is little food and many are hungry. I am not sure if you will be allowed to stay in any of the white peace towns and not be treated as slaves. This is a bad time for the Red Stick people. I am concerned for you, Little Flower and the children," Badger said, again taking the arm of Soaring Eagle.

"Thank you, you are now my friend," Soaring Eagle responded. "As you have said, I am a Red Stick Warrior. I and my family will go to the town of Horse Stealer and we will await your return with the mother of Little Flower and her family along with any others that you can set free. We will then return to the Tallapoosa. We are going home."

Chapter Fifty

Soaring Eagle and Little Flower returned to Sauwoogalooche Town. The sun rose and set five times before Badger arrived with Sun Flower Woman, Spotted Fawn, and her children. He had managed to free several other women by convincing their owners that they were only burdens and not worth the food they ate. Badger told the still outraged trader that Horse Stealer would never again return to Coweta Town.

The morning after, Soaring Eagle and Little Flower along with their children, Sun Flower Woman and fourteen others were given food and were bidden a safe travel. It was decided by Badger that Horse Stealer should leave the area, and he too joined the travelers.

Badger watched, his heart aching, as the children joyfully waved goodbye to him. The dejected warrior returned a farewell wave to Little Deer and Red Fox. He knew he would miss their excitement and curiosity. One final time, he looked deep into the soulful eyes of the beautiful Little Flower. She smiled and mouthed the words, "I am sorry." If only things had been … no, he would not allow himself to think of that. Badger had to accept that the love of Little Flower belonged to another. She had entered his life with her heart broken, now he knew it was his heart that would never heal.

Little did Soaring Eagle and his people know that long periods of time would be spent in several small villages and that their journey would be long. They would again be hungry as refuge and food were denied them many times from the white peace towns. They would suffer illness and even death, often fearing for their safety while the white soldiers still roamed the country side.

The time of new leaves would be seen four times before the weary group returned once again to the Tallapoosa. Some of the villages had been rebuilt and small groups of refugees were returning. Times had changed and life was no longer the same. The old warriors warmed by the sun, smoked their pipes, and talked of the big battle at the Horseshoe and of the days gone by.

In time, the soothing waters of the Tallapoosa healed the Hillabee people. They would find peace and happiness, again. Life would be good, but for only awhile. Then the cry of the owl filled the night with echoes of sadness from the past and yet another ominous prophecy.

The Spirit of the Red Stick Women would provide the strength needed to face and survive the dark, frightening days of the future. The days when the land they loved would no longer be their home.

The End

Epilogue

Spirit of the Red Stick Women is fiction, loosely based on actual historical facts. The account of the tragic events and the horrific battle at the Horseshoe are true. Following the battle, many of the women and children were taken as captives by the Cherokee or as in this story, taken to some of the white peace towns on the Chattahoochee and other areas. A fortunate few of the women married warriors or were adopted. The others were treated as slaves. Sadly, some may have been stoned to death. Certainly, soldiers and ruthless volunteers continued to roam the Creek countryside, eager to cause harm to any Red Stick family. Survivors regrouped and some would return to their homes.

Little Flower and her family along with Soaring Eagle and Badger, of course did not exist, or did they? It may be that a an event similar to this one did occur. We will never know. I do know that the spirit of the Red Stick women did survive and still exist to this day. I can feel it.

Debra Hughey

Acknowledgements

Books

Creek Indian Medicine Ways, The Enduring Power of Muskokee Religion, David Lewis, Jr., and Ann T. Jordan

A Historical Analysis of the Creek Indian Hillabee Towns, Don C. East

Indian Place Names in Alabama, William A. Read

Maps, Photos, Paintings and Sketches

Chattahoochee Heritage Center, Creek Indians, Fort Mitchell, Alabama

The Historical Chattahoochee Commission

Lee County Historical Society, Loachapoka, Alabama

Horseshoe Bend National Military Park

Alabama Historical Association

Historic Pensacola, Julee Cottage

The Creek, Farmers of the Southeast
Traditional Dress, Creek Woman, Okmulgee, Oklahoma
Tracey Boraas

Indians of North America, The Creeks
Michael D. Green, Frank W. Porter III, General Editor
Map of Upper and Lower Creek Towns

Personal Acknowledgements

Editing Assistance, Jeanna W. Kervin

Front Cover Sketch, Melessia Rothwein, Author's Sister

And to my husband, Fred Randall Hughey for his continuing encouragement, support, patience, time and love.

Glossary of Creek Words
And
Meanings of Towns, Place Names, Creeks and Rivers

Acee- Black Drink made from leaves of the *Lex vomitoria* plant

Huti- Creek House

Sofkee- Mush or Soup made from corn

Bear Grass- Passv or Button Snakeroot, used as medicine to reduce fever and heal sickness

Honey Locus- Kvtobwv, medicine used for disease prevention

Tallapoosa- (Early name, Oakfuskee/Fawn) Rock pulverized, little rocks, also cat in the cane break

Chattahoochee- Marked or Flowered Rocks

Saugahatchee- Turtle Rattle Creek

Oakfuskee- Point between streams; original name for Line Creek which divides current Montgomery and Macon County, Alabama

Tuckabatchee- Incorrect Town, one not sufficiently strick; Is-po-co-gee, ancient name meaning Town of Survivors

Pensacola- Choctaw for Long-haired people

Coweta- Vague ancient word having to do with eastward migration or meaning "to go"

Sauwoogalooche- Lower Creek Town, unknown meaning

Monument at Horseshoe Bend National Military Park Which Incorrectly Commemorates the Date of the Battle of Horseshoe Bend as March 29, 1814 Instead of the Documented Date of March 27, 1814.

Story Board at Horseshoe Bend National Military Park Depicting Fighting at the Barricade Between the U.S. Regulars and Militia and the Red Sticks.

Spirit of the Red Stick Women

General Andrew Jackson's Cannon Placement Overlooking the Battlefield at the Horseshoe.

Story Board at Horseshoe Bend National Military Park Depicting the Attack from the Rear of Tohopeka Village.

Spirit of the Red Stick Women

Painting at Fort Mitchell Museum Depicting U.S. Soldiers Patrolling a Path in Creek Territory, circa 1814-15.

Saugahatchee Creek Flows Over Rocks Just Below Alabama Highway 49 Bridge in Tallapoosa County.

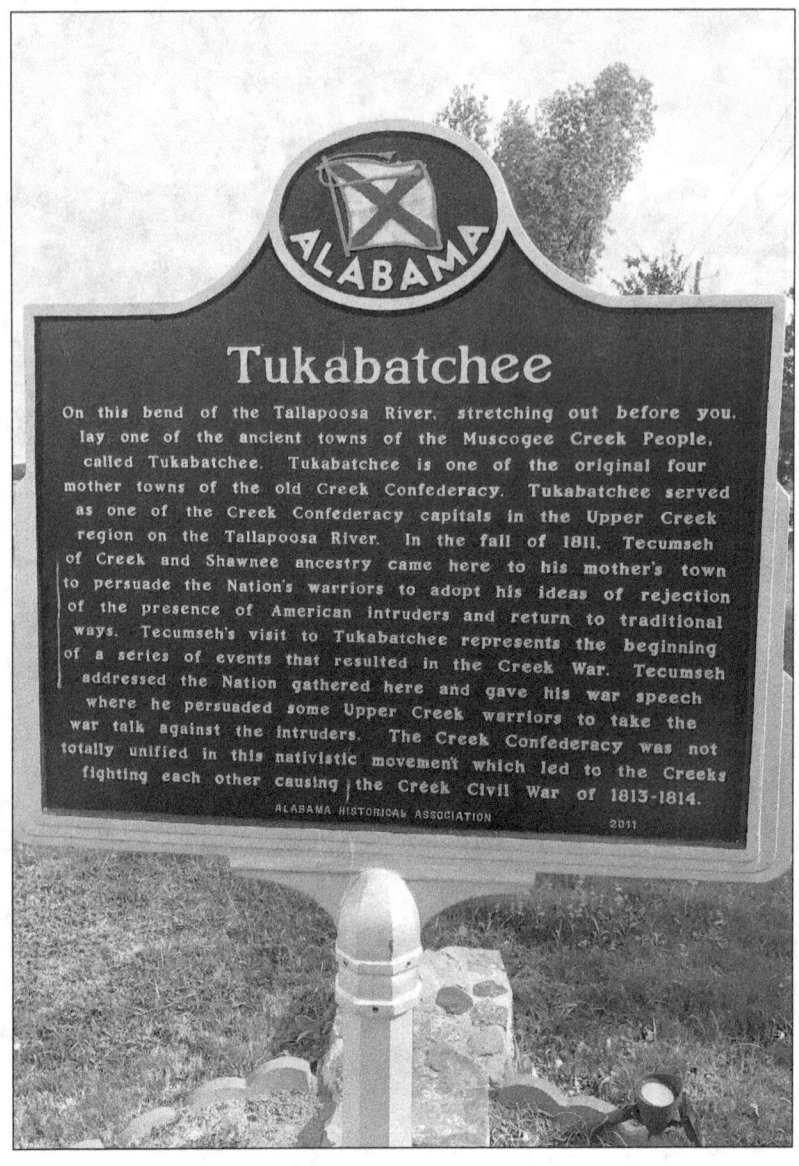

Historical Marker at the Site of Tuckabatchee on the Tallapoosa River.

Modern-Day View of Tuckabatchee Village Site Which is Now an Industrial Park and a Cotton Field.

Bridge Rock on Lower Tallapoosa River.
(Local Legend States the Creeks had a Suspension
Bridge at this Narrow Spot in the River).

Historical Marker Near the Site of Coweta Town on the Chattahoochee River.

The Author, Debra Hughey Stands Just a Few Hundred Yards From the Lower Creek Town of Coweta.

The Chattahoochee River About Two Miles Upstream from Coweta Town which was Located on the West (Right) Bank of the River.

Pete Dunaway Mural of Creek Village at Lee County Historical Society Museum in Loachapoka, Alabama.

Traditional Dress of a Creek Woman Depicted on a Granite Monument in Okmulgee, Oklahoma.

Creek Indian Attire, circa 1814-15.

Julee Cottage, an 1805 Structure Along Cobblestone Streets in Pensacola, Florida.

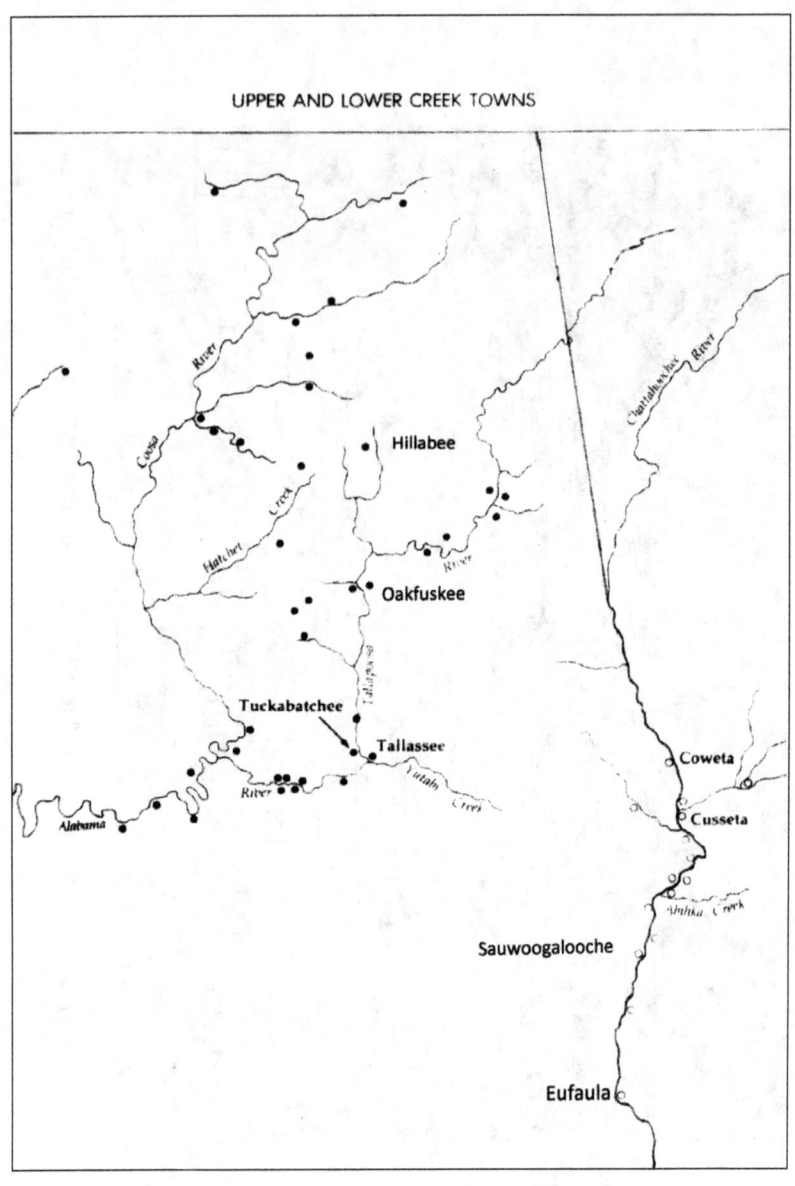

Upper and Lower Creek Towns, circa 1814-15.

www.ingramcontent.com/pod-product-compliance
Lightning Source LLC
Chambersburg PA
CBHW071620080526
44588CB00010B/1204